MIXED MARRIAGE

Between Jew and Christian

Rabbi Samuel M. Silver with Archbishop Fulton J. Sheen and Mrs. Silver.

MIXED MARRIAGE

Between Jew and Christian

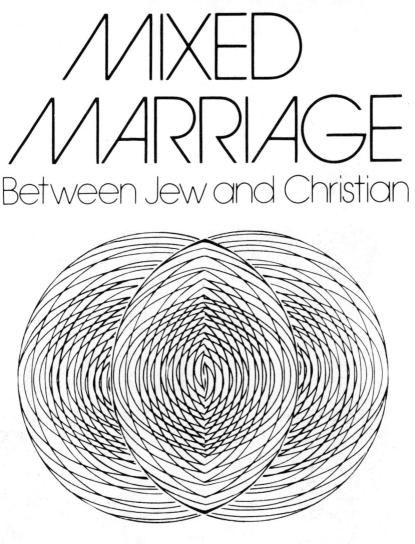

Rabbi Samuel M. Silver

ARCO PUBLISHING COMPANY INC.

219 Park Avenue South, New York, N.Y. 10003

Published by Arco Publishing Company, Inc.
219 Park Avenue South, New York, N.Y. 10003

Copyright © 1977 by Rabbi Samuel M. Silver

Library of Congress Cataloging in Publication Data

Silver, Samuel M.
  Mixed marriage between Jew and gentile.

  1. Marriage—Jews. 2. Marriage, Mixed. I. Title.

BM713.S5   296.3'87'8342   76–13004
ISBN 0–668–04046–7 (Library Edition)
ISBN 0–668–04047–5 (Paper Edition)

Printed in the United States of America

Contents

Preface

INTERMARRIAGE, MODERN STYLE

Long before Henry VIII (and after him as well), love laughed at ecclesiasts.

One of the rocks on which the Anglican church was built (by that lusty monarch, Henry) was a revolt against the norms and forms of marriage as dictated by the Roman Catholic Church. However, for all that, marriage remained a stratified phenomenon until well into our own time.

All groups, from the Indian untouchables to the lace-curtain Irish of the U.S., remained, in general, within certain confines in the area of matrimony. An out-marriage by someone of patrician blood was deemed newsworthy in all of the royal families of Europe.

In democratic America, marriage barriers were also rigidly observed. Catholics companioned Catholics, high-church Episcopalians stayed within their bounds maritally, and Jews who wandered from the faith in their choice of marriage partners were regarded as scandalous.

As for the color bar, it was mandated by miscegenation

laws in many states and enforced by a stringent tabu in the all-important realms of Hollywood and Broadway.

Now it's a new ballgame.

A number of factors has led to the explosion of intermarriage which has left many of the old school stunned, startled, and bewildered.

These factors are both admirable and deplorable.

One of them was the involvement of millions of our men in three overseas conflicts: World War II, Korea, and Indochina. Since proximity is often the chief matchmaker, the presence of so many of our men in overseas installations inevitably led to romance and in many cases, in spite of inhibiting governmental regulations, to marriage. The "war bride" became a member of American society; she was often of a different hue than her mate.

Another cause for the breakdown of the barriers against mixed marriage was the ecumenical movement. It brought together people who normally would not associate. It taught the essential equality of all groups and urged members of all faiths to respect and understand those of other outlooks. It promoted the affinity which led to countless crossovers in marriage which would have been unthinkable in an earlier era.

Permissiveness might be the name of the other factor which has accelerated the pace of intermarriage. In books, plays, and in the all-pervasive visual media of films and television, commingling was spotlighted and highlighted, and consequently emulated.

Young people who marched together in campus uprisings, antiwar demonstrations, and equal rights endeavors felt simultaneously a unity and a scorn for the restrictions against permanent marriage alliances. Many of them marched together to the altar, regardless of their denominational differences.

Still another factor in making intermarriage acceptable was the glorification of the "ethnics." Jews who were once regarded as *hors de combat* socially were now being admitted into clubs and even executive suites; matrimonial sequels were natural. The dark-skinned people, who were once shunned as "dates" and mates were also given new and higher status, and were thus qualified as acceptable marriage partners by the Wasps and other whites.

In a word, we now live in a time when the old strictures have virtually gone by the board.

Hence, it is time and most fitting to take a look at the situation. The impact of the escalating intermarriage pace has been especially jolting to the Jewish Establishment. To some Jewish leaders, the rising tide of marriages out of the faith is horrifying. Many rabbis have adopted the theme that what Hitler could not do to eliminate the Jews, intermarriage will accomplish. Similar alarm has been voiced in some Christian circles where conventional marriage arrangements seem doomed.

As in many other areas of life, those who are concerned about the survival of a group or a set of traditions will eventually come to the conclusion that in one way or another they will "have to learn to live with it."

Learning how one can "live with it" is the purpose of this book.

The Exogamy Age

In the twentieth century one has to rush to keep up with the times. It is also a chore to keep up with the terms. New words inundate our language until we begin to feel as though we were immigrants in a strange land.

Nomenclature previously unknown has become household terminology these days, often entering the other rooms through the TV den.

Think of the novel words and phrases that have been added to our language in the course of a few decades:

We are told that we now live in the Nuclear Age. In one newspaper a typographical error reversed some of the letters and it came out "Unclear Age." That's a rather accurate designation, especially for those groping with new concepts and coping with unfamiliar phenomena.

Sometimes our era is labelled "the Plastic Age," suggesting synthetics, which do indeed abound and surround us. Not all that glitters nowadays is real; much of it is artificial, both in the realms of the cosmic and cosmetic.

In another connection, we have been hailed as the first generation of the "Ecumenical Era." The word ecumenic, derived from a Greek noun, puts the stress on togetherness. The operative syllable is "cum," which in Latin means "along with." And in the ecumenical age, we are often worshipping along with people who previously were not permitted to sit close to us in religious sanctuaries.

The quipsters have been at work with these previously unknown terms. References are made in ecclesiastical circles to "ecumania," and we are told that we now have a new breed of religionist: an "ecumaniac," one who thinks any religion is better than his.

Along with the term ecumenical, we have grown accustomed to the word "ecological." In years past the meaning of that word was vague; now it's the vogue. We have been made aware of the damage done to our air, our water, and our soil. We have belatedly discovered how we have squandered fuel and other sources of energy. Little children in school know that these are days when we must pay attention to ecology. The grandparents of those youngsters would scarcely have known what ecology was; it wasn't a schoolhouse word in their time.

In a sense, this era could also be described as the Age of Exogamy.

Many people practice exogamy and don't know it. There is a character in a Molière play who, as an adult, receives his first lessons in literature. He is told the difference between prose and poetry, and then exclaims, "To think I've been talking prose all my life and didn't know it!"

Thousands of people live in a state of exogamy, but are only dimly aware of the meaning of that abstract noun, or of the extent to which they are part of a change in the mores of contemporary mankind.

Exogamy, as most of you know, means marriage out of your group. The converse is endogamy.

The grip of endogamy on most of the world's population has rarely been carefully examined, although marital inbreeding has been the hallmark of much of society throughout recorded history.

To this day when a person of royal blood marries a "commoner," it's a headlined news item. It was taken for granted—until recently—that those with blue blood were not supposed to sully their arteries by taking a partner from another, i.e., "inferior," stock.

Those with regal connections must often forfeit their claims to ascension to the throne when they contract a marriage with someone who is not of "noble" lineage. Royalty often clings to this practice even after the family has been de-throned. When there is deviation from this kind of endogamy it becomes a news flash: "a *knot* heard around the world."

We are familiar with the rigid caste system which prevailed for centuries in India. Members of certain classes there were simply "untouchable" by others, let alone marriable.

The structure of a caste system, with all its strictures, has prevailed in areas other than India. For instance, we have been told that for years the "lace-curtain Irish" would not mingle with the "shanty Irish."

The tabu against marriages outside of one's particular group has also been rigorously and vigorously enforced elsewhere. For years those who could claim that they were descendants of the early settlers of this country sought out their peers when it came time to find mates for their children.

Of course, this practice has been subjected to facetious thrusts. When an Italian was told by his neighbor that his people had come over on the Mayflower, his riposte was: "My parents came over when the immigration laws were stricter."

Strictness in the preservation of marital frontiers prevailed in many segments even in egalitarian America. For decades, Negroes and whites were forbidden by law to marry. These anti-miscegenation statutes have only recently been repealed or outlawed by court decrees.

The Montagues and the Capulets were only a few of tribes, clans, or families which kept to themselves as far as marriage was concerned.

Among the hill dwellers of Appalachia (previously called hillbillies) the feuds that frequently raged among them effectively inhibited cross-fertilization. Indeed, the poor Hatfields and McCoys were also the object of jests that had to do with marriage. One anecdote has a mountaineer scolding a nephew who "married out," predicting that the bride would "never be like kinfolk."

Without laws, the general pattern in this country was that Italians married Italians, Poles married Poles, Hungarians married Hungarians, etc. Certainly, there were many "break-outs," but by and large, endogamy was the norm for the various segments of our population.

Those who dared to defy the tabus often suffered. We know the problems which faced the Japanese and Indo-

chinese war brides brought to this country by buoyant
GI's who found passion dwindling as acceptance of their
spouses often proved nil. The lot of these brides was
almost as sad as that of the housemaid who dared to
marry a Rockefeller (a sensational alliance at the time,
but one which didn't last too long).

We may thus say that in the last decade we have indeed
entered a new epoch: the Exogamy Age. The barriers are
far from being lowered entirely, but marital crossings are
becoming more numerous all the time. We are living in a
period when even miscegenation is scarcely newsworthy.
Our films, plays, novels, and television programs have
broken free from the hitherto unwritten rules that love
must never laugh at complexion. In the population at
large, the lace Irish and the shanty Irish, and all the other
opposites of old, are getting married with hardly a raised
eyebrow.

About five years ago, a *New Yorker* magazine cartoon
showed a corpulent American patrician eyeing his daughter and her fiance, and delivering himself of a snort to the
effect, "My daughter tells me you're an ethnic!"

The ethnics and the yacht-club set are intermarrying
these days, much to the chagrin perhaps of the old-timers,
but much to the glee of the new-timers.

One group that has successfully resisted mass exogamy
more than most has been the Jewish community.

Jewish endogamy has a long history; it has been in-
wardly fostered and externally imposed for centuries.
There is nothing racial about the longtime Jewish aversion

to mixed marriage. Newcomers have always been welcomed into the Jewish fold through conversion, although proselytization has seldom been practiced.

Jewish opposition to marrying out of the group has been prompted by a desire to preserve the integrity of the Jewish religion—not the purity of Jewish blood.

To Jews, dilution of their numbers through marital defection seemed a threat to communal continuity. It was therefore taken for granted for centuries that a Jew would marry a Jew. That expectation was *de rigueur* in Jewish ranks as it was for years among Roman Catholics (or the Greek Orthodox, for that matter).

However, the general flight from endogamy has now affected the Jews. This flight has been accelerated by the change in attitude towards Jews by the gentiles.

Not so long ago it would have been regarded, in many non-Jewish quarters, a disgrace to have children maritally linked to Jews.

Even when the anti-Jewish ban was operative, gentiles realized that a Jewish boy was a "good catch." Even those who frowned on Jews secretly realized that by and large Jews were sober, honorable, and "good providers." Jewish home life was regarded as stable and the products of Jewish family life were deemed "good husbands."

In the past two score years, however, the status of the Jew has soared in the eyes of his neighbors.

Even though Hitler propagandized the world about the faults of the Jew, his virtues have come strikingly to the surface.

Many Jews are glamorous celebrities. The press gives

Jews good marks. Jewish philanthropists have won the praise of the general population. In the media, Jews and Judaism have been celebrated. "Dress British and think Yiddish," has been announced as the slogan of Madison Avenue, where many of the mores of our day are promulgated.

The Jewish religion has also been laudatorily spotlighted in novels, biographies, television specials, and feature stories. Upon examination, the Jewish faith seems more rational than others which are beclouded with obscurantism and which contain many supernatural precepts difficult to accept in a rational age and with a logical mind.

The heroism of the Jew in the heavily publicized State of Israel has also subliminally made many young people feel that it would be thrilling to be part of a great saga of human liberation.

Thus it is that gentile parents and grandparents now are less jolted when their offspring come to them to announce that they want to get married to Jews. The surge of exogamy has quickened the pace of Jewish-gentile marriages, just as it has brought about the proliferation of marital unions between Protestants and Catholics, white and black, rich and poor, etc.

Why Jews Have Shunned
Mixed Marriages

The Jews are often charged with being clannish, and the accuser will frequently base his view on the Jewish record of endogamy.

I was once pitted against the late Malcolm X on a talk show. I chided the fiery activist on his "reverse bigotry." I said that Martin Luther King Jr. had struggled for the cause of equality and had won notable victories. However, along came people like Malcolm X who began to agitate, not for desegregation, but for a new kind of separatism.

The voluble Malcolm X launched a tirade against me and the Jewish people. He scoffed at me for opposing separatism, inasmuch as "the Jews were the most clannish group in history," and had avoided mixing with other groups for centuries.

As the members of his bodyguard were nodding their heads like a set of perpendicular metronomes, Malcolm X railed at me and the "racial" track record of the Jewish people in the matter of insularity, especially with respect to closed marriages.

It was difficult for me to get a word in edgewise. No

sooner did I try to respond than I was overwhelmed by another verbal barrage.

It is true that Jews have shunned matrimonial detours, but it is important that the real reasons for this attitude be made clear.

It was not bigotry that motivated generations of Jewish parents to warn their progeny against intermarriage: it was a realistic look at the record of antisemitism. To many Jews, a gentile is either a real or potential xenophobe.

Jews are understandably moved to this attitude. For centuries the non-Jewish world subjected Jews to savage treatment. The Church in Rome vilified the Jews and made it clear to her followers that they were accursed. It was a blessing and a divine behest to mistreat them. Not only were the Jews charged with betraying their "saviour," and putting him to death, but they were also the ones who kept the world from the salvation attendant upon his putative return.

The reasoning behind this was logical to the point of being pathological: God wanted to send his Son back to earth. This Second Coming would assure the advent of an era of peace. Suffering would cease and mankind would be relieved of all of its woes. What prevented this? The Jews. Why? Because the Second Coming would not occur until the people of Jesus accepted Him. The Jews, made aware of this situation, adamantly refused to acknowledge him. Who, then, was to blame for the continued per-sistence in the world of poverty, of strife, of evil? The Jews. Hence it was the divinely ordained mission of the Church to subject anyone tainted with Jewishness to the rack. The Inquisition was a way of purging people of their Judaic blemish.

I must hasten to aver that in recent times the Catholic Church has given up this twist in their theological dogma. The Protestant Church has also relinquished this point of view.

However, for centuries the Jew was treated as a pariah, locked up into ghettos, regarded as tainted, branded as a deicide. No wonder the Jews were constrained to look upon the non-Jew with fear and apprehension!

Shakespeare never met a Jew, but he had heard about them through the Medieval grapevine which pictured the people of Moses in such horrid hues. Hence it was easy for Shakespeare to fortify the stereotypes that reached him. It would have been odd for Shakespeare to depict the Jew other than in hateful terms, for he knew no better. It was miraculous that Shakespeare was able to find in his heart a bit of compassion for the odious Jew, but in general his "Shylock" reinforced the common belief that the Jew was guilty of all the characteristics attributed to him. It was natural for Shakespeare to label his drama in which the Jew is stripped of his wealth and his lovely daughter as a "comedy."

Shylock's concern over the loss of his daughter to a non-Jew becomes more comprehensible when we view the world from the ghetto. The gentile was the enemy, the persecutor, the tormentor; for no valid reason he went out of his way to stigmatize the Jew. How could a Jewish parent regard the marriage of his child to an enemy with equanimity?

Oddly enough, in the pre-Christian era, the Jewish attitude towards intermarriage was mixed. True, there are Biblical warnings against mingling with outsiders, especially when the latter were implacable foes bent on the extinction of the Israelites. The peoples who refused to permit Moses and the Israelites to pass through their land, even though Moses promised that his people would do no harm, were proscribed as suitable marriage mates. The ancient Hebrews were forbidden to consort with idolaters lest the purity of the faith (not the purity of the race) were to be diminished.

Despite the strictures in the Bible against intermarriage, however, almost all the great personages of Jewish Scriptures did go outside their group maritally. The wife of Moses was an Ethiopian. Joseph married the daughter of an Egyptian nobleman. Esther, who saved her people, was urged to marry the King of Persia by her devout cousin, Mordecai. Solomon, glorified as the wisest of men, was wedded to dozens of non-Jews. Ruth, the ancestress of King David, from whose loins the Messiah was to come, was a Moabite woman.

It is true that Ezra chastised all Jews who had intermarried and actually importuned them to give up their non-Hebraic spouses. However, it is questionable whether his suggestion was carried out, and even post-Biblical Jewish individuals of prominence contracted marriages outside of the faith.

Then the long, dark night of Medievalism, with its tragic downgrading of the Jew, made him wary of becoming involved in interfaith marriages.

The same record of anti-Jewish hostility has extended to modern times. Malcolm X would not let me break into his monologue long enough to explain that many American-Jewish parents and grandparents sighed with anguish when their young people announced their desire to marry out of the faith because they remembered the attitude and acts of gentiles in Eastern Europe.

The persecution of the Middle Ages continued in Czarist Russia (and has not ceased in Bolshevik Russia, although the pogroms are now "cold" ones). Under the Russian rulers, ghettos were continued, with the Jews limited to residences within the "Pale," i.e., fixed boundaries. Butchery and savagery against the Jews was a constant pattern in Russian life. These acts of oppression were officially countenanced and were often instigated by the government or by the Orthodox religious authorities.

Pretend that you are a Jewish grandmother. Your recollection of gentiles in Russia was that of people breaking into your home, ravishing or ravaging your people, and destroying your possessions. Your recollection of the "outsider" was of one who looked at you with unrelieved hatred. You know that you were condemned and mistreated only because you were Jewish. Now you live in America. Your granddaughter or grandson comes to you and says, "I'm in love with a Christian." The word "Christian" triggers a flashback of horror. Do you think that you could contemplate your offspring being embraced by a Christian with ease of mind? Hardly.

True, in the U.S. pogroms had no vogue, but it was difficult for Jewish fathers and mothers to accustom themselves to the idea that a non-Jew could be anything but a potential persecutor.

Perhaps I can dramatize the problem with an example from my own family. My late father was a native of Rumania, a country with a brutal history of antisemitism. My father's father had owned some land in Rumania when that country was under Turkish rule. When Rumania broke away from the Ottoman Empire, the first order of business of the new regime was to expropriate farms from the Jews: they weren't "worthy" of owning any part of the soil of the Fatherland.

Jew-hatred was often vicious in Rumania. My father's grimmest memories had to do with the celebration of Easter. When that holiday was observed, when the resurrection of the "meek lamb, Jesus" was being commemorated, the priests in the sanctuary regaled the worshippers with detailed descriptions of the death of the Saviour. With the description of the shedding of each drop of the blood of Jesus, the blood of the worshipper was ignited. By the time the crucifixion was re-enacted, the insides of the worshipper were churning. Some of the most terrible assaults on the Jews occurred immediately after the Easter devotions. My father told me that Jews would huddle in their basements (if they had them in their wretched hovels) or in caves or other hideaways, tremulously awaiting the exodus from the churches at Eastertide. If no violence occurred, it was deemed a miracle.

A generation later, my father's son, a rabbi in the United States, would often be invited to address Christian congregations on Easter. In an Episcopalian Church I was the featured speaker every noon for a week at Holy Week services. I have often gone to Catholic churches and have staged full-dress Passover services, explaining that Jesus was celebrating that Jewish holiday at the Last Supper.

Yes, America *is* different, and much progress has been made in recent generations. However, despite the change, can anyone imagine how my father would have reacted if one of his children or grandchildren had come to him and said, "Dad, I'm going to marry a gentile." Try to conceive what the term "gentile" would mean to my father.

This is not all. The link between gentile and cruelty did not cease with the downfall of Czarist Russia and the emigration of millions of Jews from Eastern Europe to the friendlier shores of America.

Let's focus on the Hitler period. By a 99 percent vote of its electorate, continental Europe's most enlightened nation elevated a 100 percent antisemite to its highest office. Long before he was voted into office, Hitler revealed his beliefs and intentions. One of his views was that the Jew was irretrievably damned. The Church had granted the Jew an "out," saying that if the Jew would repent of his obduracy and be baptized he could deliver himself of his stigma.

Hitler made no such concession. Not in the Middle Ages, but in modern times, he declared war on the Jew, branding him as irredeemable.

How did the gentile world react to Hitler's declaration? Was there a tremor of repugnance? Hardly. The U.S. kept trading with him, exchanging diplomatic niceties. The Vatican condemned birth controllers and Communists, but did not excommunicate Hitler, although he was ostensibly a Roman Catholic communicant; indeed, the Vatican established a Concordat with the Butcher. The Protestant Church in Germany accepted Hitler, with a few exceptions. In other nations, the churches raised no objections to his vile theses. Indeed, even America did not withdraw its ambassador and probably would have gone on recognizing Hitler in spite of his death camps. War came only because Hitler's ally struck us at Pearl Harbor.

The Holocaust is a word loosely bandied about these days. It meant the systematic slaughter of millions of people, including innocent children. It also reflected global apathy over the fate of the Jews. Many would counter with the assertion that the Negroes have also suffered. They have, but they were not confronted with methodical extermination. They were the victims of indifference and exploitation, of bigotry and discrimination, but they were also the playthings of hypocrisy: the U.S. Constitution ostensibly forbade mistreatment because of color or place of origin. In the case of the Hitler onslaught, the Jews were targeted only because they were Jews, and the civilized world gazed at the barbarian and lifted not a finger to stop him.

This is the only background against which we can sit in judgment on Jewish parents confronted with the prospect of having a gentile marry a member of their family. A number of books have been written condemning both Jews and gentiles for their opposition to intermarriage, and the writers have hurled plagues on both houses. However, it is doubtful whether the Jewish reaction to intermarriage should be bracketed with the feelings of gentiles whose noses were put out of joint over the prospect of acquiring an "ethnic" daughter- or son-in-law. The two attitudes are hardly similar. One derives from a gruesome historical record; the other is sheer snobbishness.

Another factor to be considered in trying to penetrate the mind of the Jewish parents is the Hebrew tradition of family life. Jewish parents look forward eagerly to expanding their circle of affection through the acquisition of "machetanim."

Machetanim (you pronounce it with a gargle) is a word lacking in English. It denotes the parents of your daughter- or son-in-law. The masculine singular is mechutan. The feminine is machetayneste. Which recalls a happening:

In the halcyon days of the Nixon Administration, a Bulgarian-born Jew who became an affluent builder in Florida decided to stage the Bar Mitzvah of his son in Israel and to take his guests there by plane. On his payroll was John Eisenhower, the son of the late President. In Israel, he was introduced as Nixon's mechutan, since his son was married to Nixon's daughter. When he first heard the word, Eisenhower said, "I'm what?" The word was explained. He later toured Israel and wherever he went he would introduce himself not by name but by the announcement, "I'm Nixon's mechutan."

It is the dream of most Jewish families to have machetanim with whom they have rapport. The machetanim become part of the extended family circle. They are proudly introduced to the relatives and are absorbed into one's life.

In general, Jews mingle freely even when they are strangers. The same likemindedness characterizes any group with commonalty. Let two Americans meet in Europe and instantly they are welded together. However, when Jewish families confront non-Jewish machetanim the spell doesn't work: there is strangeness, there is alienation, and with Jewish families who pride themselves on their adherence, there is often acute embarrassment.

Given this background, we can readily see what a wrench the discovery of an outfaith marriage in one's family can produce in the hearts of Jewish parents.

To equate this attitude with that of the non-Jew is not quite accurate. The non-Jew is frequently guilty of hatred. The Jewish parents described above feel shame, but not hostility. The record of gentile treatment of the Jew has often been bloody, while the attitude towards the non-Jew is a matter of embarrassment.

There is a world of difference between them.

Malcolm X would not stop talking long enough for these considerations to be submitted. And the young couples who encounter opposition from their parents, Jewish and non-Jewish, are much too engrossed in their own passions to sort out the variations between the reaction of the Jewish side and the gentile side.

However, these are the facts, and a decent regard for the accumulated feelings of the Jewish parents should be forthcoming.

Obstacles to Intermarriage

(Or, Why It Is Safer to Stay Maritally with Your Own Group)

If you're smart, you'll marry someone in your own group.

When young people, ignited with passion, are the recipients of this kind of advice, they bristle. How, they want to know, can people be so intolerant? They insist that love can't be cribbed or confined.

Of course, reasoning with those inflamed with romance is exceedingly difficult. Couples bent on marriage across religious or racial divisions tend to regard warnings about the future of their relationship as bigotry.

To them such counsel is like the old cinema rules which forbade the showing of a white man embracing a Negro girl, or vice versa. They pigeonhole it as old-fashioned little-mindedness on the part of those who want to retain views that are dated and antiquated.

The proper time to consider the consequences of exogamy is not when passion is high, but when rational considerations prevail.

A case can be made against mixed marriage which does

not smack of that phenomenon called "the dislike of the unlike." The arguments against intermarriage can be based on sheer pragmatism. In fact, they can be reduced to plain statistics.

If you contemplate the aftermath of such marriages, you may well be stunned into endogamy. The divorce rate in our nation is incredibly high: Marriages fail in the U.S. in a ratio of one to four. Intermarriages collapse on a one to two scale!

In other words, your decision to enter into a marital relationship with someone of a different faith or race means that you are gambling with your future well-being.

The tragedy of divorce is not diminished by its high frequency. The inroads on the nervous system of those who have loved and lost are incalculable. There are also inroads on one's financial resources. A couple I know are at odds with one another, and have nothing to do with one another, but they are still technically married because "we can't afford a divorce."

Must we discuss the shattering impact of a divorce when children are involved? When youngsters watch their parents drift apart, the effect is searing. The bewilderment they experience is virtually unrecountable.

Those who produce life should not destroy life. A couple which engenders children and then endangers them by their reckless disregard of one another and their offspring are guilty of a terrible offense.

The time to think of the possibility of such a disaster would be long before one is enamored of someone. The proper time is before one is involved in a serious romance.

Numerous instances of broken marriages occurred due to the tumult of war. GI's in the Pacific theater of war were often stationed in lands where feminine companionship was a rare phenomenon. The cynical, albeit bigoted, comment often made was something to the effect that "I've been on this rock so long that the natives have begun to look white."

In such circumstances liaisons with residents of those islands became commonplace. Such casual connections often blossomed into true affection and marriages were contracted. The GI discovered that his foreign mate was a girl of exemplary character, and her attractiveness made marriage a most desirable objective. And so they were married. After the war, the bride came to the States. Soon the couple was subjected to pinpricks. Eventually, these became unbearable. Well adjusted when they were overseas, the couple then became aware of their differences. Thousands of such alliances ended up in the divorce courts. The fate of the multi-hued progeny is frequently a dismal one.

When the marital crossover is religious, the same sad ending too often occurs. In my study, I have seen Jewish-Christian pairs at every stage. I have seen them at the dating stage, the courting stage, the engagement stage, the marriage stage, the baby-blessing stage, the quarreling stage, and the break-up stage.

I can remember cautioning such a couple that there might be trouble if a Jew marries a gentile. Sitting there in my office, with their hands intertwined, they looked at me with more pity than anger. How could I dare to suggest that the bond which held them together would ever be weakened! I married them. They lived happily together for two years. Then the normal little hassles began; nothing serious, just mildly irritating problems. Then one morning, after a quarrel, the gentile sat up in bed and said, "That's what I get for marrying a goddam Jew!"

Imbroglios of this kind are deftly handled in the world of humor. One story has it that the son of a Jewish businessman became entranced by a "shiksa" (gentile girl) and told his father he was going to marry her.

"If you do, there'll be trouble," warned the father.

Oh no, oh-noed the son. She was going to convert to Judaism.

After the honeymoon, the father telephoned his son and told him to hurry over to the store because it was full of customers.

"I can't come to the store today," explained the young man. "It's Saturday."

"Of course it is. That's why we're so busy. Come in a hurry."

"I can't," explained the son. "My wife won't let me." (Having been instructed by an Orthodox rabbi, the newly Judaized wife insisted that her husband observe the Sabbath by abstaining from labor.)

"I told you," shouted the enraged father, "that there would be trouble if you married a shiksa."

The opposite of this story is the one where the Jewish boy, out of love for his Catholic fiancee, took instructions in Catholicism with her parish priest.

The process was so successful that the marriage had to be cancelled. The pupil became so intrigued with Catholicism that he decided to become a priest!

And who does not remember the classical riposte of Sammy Davis Jr., who, at the golf club, was asked what his handicap was, and responded: "I'm colored, I'm Jewish, and I have only one eye."

Then there's the tale about Marilyn Monroe and Elizabeth Taylor gossiping about another actress, with one of them offering the tidbit: "Well, what can you expect of a shiksa?"

Speaking of Monroe, they say that she was once invited to be the guest of honor at an interfaith dinner "because she has had a husband of each of the three faiths."

The grim truth is (and the Monroe and Taylor experiences verify it) that those who enter into an intermarriage have a hard row to hoe. The normal difficulties of adjustment that a couple faces in order to synchronize their lives successfully are greatly exacerbated if their backgrounds are diverse. No amount of protestation can annul this fact. After all, that model romantic of literature, Romeo, was susceptible to Juliet immediately after another romantic dalliance which he was certain would prove lasting.

A marriage will prove lasting, on balance, if there is commonalty between husband and wife. The greater the disparity, the greater the hazards. Whenever one makes this statement, one must add the obligatory concession, "Yes, I know that many intermarriages work well. I, too, know many couples who have made a go of the mix."

However, on a percentage basis, the discreet individual concerned about his own welfare would do well to marry one of his own faith.

Some clergymen will consent to officiate at a mixed marriage providing that the couple will pledge to raise possible future children in the faith to which that clergyman adheres. The rationale for this insistence is the desire to secure the next generation for one's denomination.

In my own case, I make no such demand. This is not to say that I am indifferent to the well-being either of my religious group or of the offspring of the intermarriage.

As a matter of fact, the offspring are often the chief sufferers from exogamy.

No matter what religious decision a couple with differing backgrounds makes, the children are victimized and are subjected to handicaps and problems. As I often put it, "No matter what you do about future children, it won't work well."

Let us imagine, for example, that a Catholic boy wants to marry a Jewish girl. After serious thought over the religious aspect of their future, they decide that one home is only big enough for one faith. The Jew decides to convert to Catholicism.

Ultimately they are blessed with a child. The child is reared in the Catholic Church. It won't take long for that youngster to realize that there is something fragmentary about the Catholicism of his family unit. One set of grandparents are among the faithful, but the other set are "outsiders." As Jews, they are not eligible for many of the benefits which Catholics enjoy during their lifetime and after it. The youngster mingles with peers who are fully Catholic on both sides of their family. He begins to feel a bit strange. This strangeness is deepened when he makes more contact with the Jews in his orbit: the grandparents, uncles, cousins, aunts, etc.

Should the couple have decided to "go Jewish," the same results would ensue. The child discovers that one set of grandparents is a "Christmas tree," and the other is a "Chanukah light." He begins to feel as though he were different from his contemporaries.

Or the couple may opt to remain unaffiliated with any religion. They proceed along the ostensibly logical course of "letting our children decide for themselves what they want to be." This brave resolution is often accompanied by the determination "to expose our children to all religions and then let the choice be theirs." This can be the most illogical alternative. Little children should be warmly integrated into a religion. When they are very young, they are not qualified to pick a faith any more than they are fit to pick their own diets or wardrobes, and the impact of a religion is greatest when little ones are naturally reared in it. Exposing juveniles to a variety of religions can only confuse them. When children view the sancta within a home from their earliest years they become accustomed to them and naturally "take" to them. If they are allowed to see one set of customs and then another and asked to pick the one they like best, their reactions are usually born out of bewilderment and not out of a natural affinity for the practices of their parents.

Furthermore, a youngster wants to "belong." It does not

matter what group he's in, but he wants to be part of an established group. Imagine a cluster of children who have somehow gotten around to the question of religion:

"What are you?" one is asked.

"I'm Catholic," is the reply.

Around and around the query goes. Finally, it is the turn of the unaffiliated child. Confused, he can only answer the question, "What are you?" with the reply, "I'm nothing."

Whereupon he is stigmatized with the most devastating of all epithets, "Oddball!"

The traumatic effects of such an experience are dreadful. It is pathetic that such effects can derive from an honest and earnest desire on the part of the parents to be "fair" to their child, to permit him to "decide for himself" which religion to adopt.

Aside from the problem of what to do about the children, the couple will make a startling discovery. Young people sometimes gravitate towards partners of another faith because their own faith means little to them. They reason, "My religion isn't that important to me, so why should I hesitate to go out with someone of another religion?" However, when their lives become intertwined with a partner of a different background, such individuals learn that the topic which they would like to keep submerged looms up and intrudes into the picture.

Indeed, to these minimalists religion often becomes a third partner in their relationship. When Christian youngsters announce their choice to parents and grandparents, they must add, "But he's a Jew." This produces a scowl or a growl. When they plan their ceremony, the matter of religion often becomes a dominant consideration as they discuss how they should be married and by whom. The Jewish partner (who may have successfully avoided the rabbi for years) now suddenly finds himself in the synagogue study, describing the extent of his devoutness. Often the same couple finds it necessary to shuttle between clergymen for the sake of the feelings of the older generation. In imparting the glad news of their engagement, the couple find themselves ensnarled willy-nilly in discussions about religion. They have professed themselves indifferent to the religious aspect of their bond but, more and more, that aspect becomes "Topic A."

After leaping over the hurdle of the marriage ceremony, the religious specter is not downed.

The life of an intermarried couple is haunted by religious matters, or related ones.

The Christian girl married to a Jew quickly learns how immature our society is. She learns that people will cut her off because she is a wife of a Jew. She learns that some people do not want her in their apartment houses because her husband is a Jew. She learns that her husband is handicapped in his quest for a job because he is a Jew.

She learns that she is denied membership in a country club or a yacht club because of the Jewish taint. Even the wife of Richard Rodgers voiced a plaint of this kind in one of the women's magazines not long ago. She learns that even some garden clubs do not want her in their ranks because she is not sufficiently "Waspy." She tastes the bitterness of being excluded from all kinds of groups and organizations and circles.

Groucho Marx put it facetiously once when he was supposed to have said at the refusal of a swim club to let him become a member, "My daughter is only half-Jewish. Please let her swim in your pool up to her navel."

Whatever the intermarried couple does there are occasions of discomfiture. If they are at an all-Jewish social gathering, the others may employ some Yiddishisms which the Christian wife doesn't understand. If the others don't know she's a "shiksa," they may be guilty of comments which will discomfort her. If they do know, her presence will introduce a note of awkwardness to the gathering: it is hard to relax when a stranger is in your midst.

Precisely the same situation prevails when the shoe is on the other religious foot. In our imaginary couple, the Jewish consort of a gentile woman is mingling with an all-"goyish" group. If they are not aware of his background, he may be stung by some of the remarks that may be dropped, not necessarily antisemitic but moderately deprecatory, such as the comment on the part of someone that he was negotiating the price of something and then "I tried to Jew him down."

If the all-gentile company is notified that Mr. X is of Jewish descent (a favorite term used by Henry Kissinger), a pall is cast over the party. There is none of the unbuttoned ease which characterizes the casual togetherness of a likeminded group.

Here again, religion, which was something the couple wanted to play down, rears its unwanted head.

The same unwelcome subject breaks into the mixed home with greater insistence when Holiday Time comes around. What does such a couple do at Christmas time? Do they have a tree, or don't they? Do they decorate the house or its lawn, or don't they?

Numerous are the episodes fraught with ill-will during the holiday season in mixed marriages! Christian in-laws will ask their daughter, "Aren't you celebrating Christmas?" She must give reply, "I'd better not. Joe wouldn't like it." Should Joe go along with Christmas he will more often than not get raised eyebrows from his side of the family. "Joe, how could you, the grandson of a rabbi, have a Christmas tree in your house!"

Easter is another problem. No matter how tenuous the hold of piety on the Christian partner there is a church-ward tug when the season of the resurrection arrives.

"If not for my sake, at least for the sake of my parents, Joe, come to church with us for the Easter service?" the wife may plead.

Say that Joe goes. Does he kneel, if the service is Catholic, or doesn't he? If the entire family group kneels and Joe doesn't, isn't he "making a scene?" What happens when Joe's Jewish parents hear that he attended an Easter mass? Doesn't Joe know that Easter involves doctrines and ideas alien to Jews, sometimes hostile to Judaism?

The Jewish holy days offer further intrusions into the life of the couple to whom religion meant little. Will Christine go to the synagogue with Joe's family for the observances which no Jew misses, the New Year and the Day of Atonement? If Christine does attend, doesn't she feel strange there? And isn't everyone looking at them? There have been occasions when the Christine in question was wearing a crucifix about her neck, not necessarily out of devoutness but just for adornment. The sight of the non-Jewish girl in the temple pew is enough to distract other worshippers from concentrating on their prayers or listening to the cantor or the rabbi. Passover can also bring problems.

One couple I know were at sword's point because the gentile wife insisted on having a picture of Jesus in the bedroom. She wasn't doing it because of her attachment to the Christian Savior but out of sentimental devotion to her late grandmother who bequeathed the family heirloom to her in her last will and testament. The sparks flew for a long time, embroiling the couple, the in-laws, the neighbors and the respective confidants of each of the embattled pair.

Any clergyman or, for that matter, any family in which an intermarriage has occurred can go on for hours, detailing the complications ensuing from a marital mix. The situation is just as intricate when it is race and not religion which divides the partners and threatens their harmony.

Yes, many intermarriages work out well and modern society is full of examples of such successful matings. However, the success of such marriages frequently reflects dexterity in a tightrope operation.

There is no doubt that a couple which frankly faces the pitfalls of such a union will be able to cope with them better than one which blindly ignores them.

Indeed, to look at the other side for a moment, some intermarriages work well because the couple astutely transforms obstacles into stepping-stones. That is to say, they squarely face the problem and make it a point to combat it. They make a game of the situation. They adopt a policy which I have reduced to a verbal formula: "Instead of letting certain things irritate you, let them amuse you."

Such couples enhance their life together by making overcoming the obstacles a project challenging their resourcefulness as well as their sense of humor. This idea gives additional zest to their marriage.

One couple I know utilized an original play, or ploy. The Jewish husband didn't look it; the gentile wife had an appearance which seemed more Jewish. When the husband would hobnob with other men and whenever the talk got somewhat xenophobic, he would say, "I wish you wouldn't talk that way. I haven't told you before, but it happens that my wife is Jewish." The slurs would cease, but the atmosphere was still charged with awkwardness.

To overcome the hurdles attendant on intermarriage demands a great effort. To sustain the effort in the teeth of the normal wear and tear on romance as passion subsides and the daily chore of adjustment takes place requires as much deliberate care as keeping love itself in high gear.

So I go back to my original thesis. Learning to love someone of another faith is relatively easy. Learning to live with such an individual is more difficult. Those who cross religious lines are frequently those to whom religion means little. However, what happens in a religious crossover is that the very subject which the couple would like to ignore is the one which begins to preoccupy them more and more.

Looked at objectively, the person to whom religion is of little moment should marry someone of his own persuasion. When two Christians of little piety marry, religion hardly ever needs to be discussed. Oh yes, there's the matter of the wedding ceremony and a few times a year one bows in the direction of the church. For most of the year, their desire to play down religious matters can easily be gratified.

Thus two Jews who never darken the threshold of a synagogue may marry and have little occasion to think about religion. Oh yes, on state occasions, a few times during the year, they pay a courtesy call on the temple. For the rest of the year, the matter can readily be suppressed or kept out of sight.

However, when those whose devoutness is minimal espouse someone of another faith, the matter of religion becomes annoyingly chronic, and often explosive!

How Mixed Couples Are Joined: The Ceremony

In this age of ecumenism we have all become witnesses to the ritual ceremonies of faiths other than our own.

There was a time when most Christians hadn't the dimmest idea of what a Bar Mitzvah looked like. Today, many Christians have attended a Bar Mitzvah service. Indeed, they tell about a heavily Judaized suburb of New York where virtually the whole town turns up every Saturday morning at the local synagogue for the Bar Mitzvah of one of the thirteen-year-old residents. When a member of the Christian minority of the town was approaching his thirteenth birthday, he was asked what he wanted for the occasion. Naturally, he responded, "a Bar Mitzvah."

Nor can you blame the youngster. The Bar Mitzvah boy often walks away with so many presents that one father complained that his boy wouldn't talk to him at the end of the day because, "I don't like to mingle with people in the lower income brackets."

Just as Christians are now familiar, in large numbers, with the inside of a synagogue because of the popularity of Bar Mitzvahs, so Jews have become accustomed to sitting in churches for baptisms, weddings, funeral masses, and even regular worship services in this interfaith age.

It is this new commingling, so typical of the Age of Ecumenism, that has accelerated the pace of intermarriage.

In previous times, when there was a sharp division among the various religious groupings, the possibility of crossing religious lines in quest of a spouse was almost unthinkable. It was a seldom phenomenon. Nowadays, it is a daily occurrence.

We might pause a bit and contemplate the background and significance of the new ecumenism.

For centuries Jews and Christians were isolated from one another. The division was odd since Judaism and Christianity have much in common, as much as a mother and a daughter. Beginning as an offshoot of Judaism, Christianity moved farther and farther away from it. When Christianity was able to win over the Roman Imperial family, the entire Western world became a Christian preserve.

Christians often ask why the Jews didn't accept Jesus. However, the only ones who did accept him were Jews, inasmuch as his original followers and disciples were all Jewish. What separated the two groups was a metamorphosis in Christianity itself; it began as the religion *of* Jesus and ended up being the religion *about* Jesus.

The religion of Jesus was Judaism. True, he was critical of some of the leaders, but no more so than the Biblical prophets. The schism occurred when St. Paul and his successors, the Church Fathers, elevated Jesus into the realm of divinity. Judaism teaches that all of us are children of

God, but that none of us is on the same echelon as the Deity.

Paulinian theology introduced a new element, the apotheosis—that is, the deification of Jesus along with another mystical partner, the Holy Spirit. Trinitarianism is a belief that can inspire noble behavior, but it is a departure from the Jewish idea of the absolute indivisibility of the godhead.

Beneath the theological differences of Judaism and Christianity, or perhaps above them, there is still a core of common ideas. Both faiths subscribe to the conviction that there is a Force or a Source of life which is intangible but real. Both faiths recommend a style of living which stresses morality. Both faiths derive inspiration from the Jewish Bible and its spiritual protagonists. Both faiths make use of the same Psalms when they are engaged in prayer. Both faiths envisage a better society, one radiant with human harmony and the cessation of strife. Both have ecclesiastical organizations which are parallel in structure and strictures.

The long period of bloody oppression visited by Christians on Jews eventuated from an idea, gradually being rejected in modern times, that the failure of the Jew to recognize the salvation offered by Jesus was the cause for the delay of the Second Coming. The Jew was blamed for the perpetuation of evil in the world, because were he not so stubborn and were he to avow a belief in Jesus a spiritual utopia would descend upon the world. The notion that the Jew was obstinate led to the belief that he was accursed. To make him aware of his blindness became, to some, an obligation and a spur to persecution. In some quarters, the aim of the persecution was to compel the Jew to see the error of his ways and to embrace Christianity, since this would hasten the gladsome day of human redemption.

Upon such premises the cruel system associated with Inquisitions, pogroms, and ghettos arose. The toll in suffering and death is incalculable, and some assert that there is a straight line between the torment of the Jew under the Church and the hounding of the Jew under Hitler.

As a consequence of being reduced to pariah status, the Jew, in his sequestered ghettos, built up a defense against his lot. He could not physically do battle with his cruel persecutors who, in the name of a gentle Savior, were exceedingly ungentle. The Jew was able to endure his sad lot by telling himself that those who mistreated him were spiritually immature and that they had not yet fully learned the lessons of good behavior. It was imcumbent upon the Jew, his rabbis taught him, to be patient, to be scholarly, to be devout, and to have faith in the ultimate rectification of the injustice in the world.

That the Jew was able to preserve his equanimity over the long centuries of suffering is almost incredible. No wonder a philosopher once replied to· a monarch who demanded proof that God could accomplish miracles with the simple rejoinder, "The Jews, sire."

In our day, the change in the Christian attitude towards the Jew has been spectacular. There were always Christian scholars who remonstrated with their fellows against the brutality of persecution. Some of those learned men made some headway, but it required the savagery of the Nazis to bring the Christian world to its senses. Revulsion against Hitler was followed by admiration for the valor of the fighting Jews in Israel. In the meanwhile, in the U.S. armed forces during the World War II, another quiet revolution took place.

Hundreds of rabbis were in the Army and the Navy. These rabbis came into close contact with Christian GI's. The U.S. Government itself was an ecumenical force, since it stipulated that a chaplain was spiritually responsible for men in his group no matter what their religion. So it often happened that a rabbi would conduct worship services of a general nature, and give counsel to non-Jews. It also often happened that a Christian chaplain was obligated to lead devotions for Jewish men.

The religious interaction in World War II led to a new appreciation and understanding of the other man's faith, unlike anything which had ever been known before.

During World War II I was a passenger on a troop ship which carried 1500 men. I was the only clergyman. Army regulations mandated me to look after the spiritual needs of the men in my area. I recruited a choir and had Protestant prayers mimeographed and each Sunday, during a long stretch and hang-up between the Hawaiian and the Philippine Islands, I conducted the services for the Protestant men. Indeed, the entire ship became a church as my choristers and I stood topsail and guided the congregation from our lofty perch with amplifiers.

I could not actually perform a mass for the Catholic men, but I mimeographed the prayers, secured a Catholic officer who led the others in the rosary, and each Sunday

and day of obligation delivered a homily to the men
gathered on the fantail. I then asked the ship's carpenter
to fashion a crucifix for the Catholic gathering. And aboard
that ship and in dozens of letters sent home there was comment about "the Jewish rabbi who got the Protestant
ship's carpenter to make a crucifix for Catholic services."

On the other side of the coin, ponder this. I was stationed on a Philippine island called Leyte. To minister to
the Jewish men I was always on the go, visiting various
outposts of the island and some of its "suburbs." My
Sabbath schedule was so crowded that I would conduct
"Friday night services" every other Tuesday night on a
nearby island called Samar. The Seabees of that island
then went to a Protestant chaplain stationed there and
asked him to alternate with me. He knew some Hebrew
and gladly consented. I had some conferences with him,
and he became the interim "rabbi" for the Jewish group.

Once a Seabee came up to me after I had conducted
the service and said, "Chaplain, I like the other rabbi
better than you." I asked why, and the reply was, "He's
more Orthodox than you are."

That is not an untypical illustration of the religious side
of that unfortunate interlude known as World War II.
There is no doubt that such happenings were a cause of
the postwar ecumenical surge.

The first to formalize the process of interreligious com-
radeship were the Protestants who broke precedent by
inviting the Vatican to send observers to a gathering of
the World Council of Churches in Christ held some years
ago in New Delhi. That made it easy for the Vatican to

reciprocate later when the historic Vatican Council was convoked by the now almost legendary Pope John.

Pope John was so liberal in his outlook that conservatives branded his encyclicals "sickles" cum hammer. Pope John figuratively mounted this world of ours on his frail shoulders and pointed it in an entirely new direction. He spearheaded the new Ecumenical Epoch, and the end is not yet. His successor has slowed the pace somewhat, but not decisively; Pope Paul visited Israel and the U.S. where his plea before the UN asking for peace was much in the spirit of Pope John.

Pope John's doings were spectacular. He greeted a large Jewish delegation from the U.S. in Hebrew. He came down from his throne, with hands extended, and said: *"Ah-nee Yosayph achee-chem"* ('I am Joseph, your brother'). His Vatican Council reversed a millennia of antagonism against the Jew, telling the world of the remorse felt by the sensitive Catholics over the unfair and cruel mistreatment of the Jews by the followers of Jesus. He established unprecedented rapport with Protestants, with the Eastern Orthodox Church, and even with Communist countries.

Another John, whose surname was Kennedy, was simultaneously making new inroads against intergroup hostility in the U.S. As the first Catholic president of our union, his outlook, his catholicism with a small c, and his daring assaults on bigotry further advanced the cause of good feeling among people of diverse religious backgrounds.

As the world contemplated the brief but significant "reigns" of the two Johns, it experienced a reduction of intergroup hostility. The world suddenly became more unified. The after-effects of this period are still being registered, and it became a decided factor in the area of marriage, making young people amenable to joining in marriage with those of different backgrounds.

Another force for bringing people together was the civil rights crusades led by Martin Luther King Jr. and the aftermath of his demonstrations: campus uprisings of all kinds in which young people were brought together in movements on behalf of many causes. As they marched together under common banners it became easier for them to march together down the middle aisle.

The result of this new feeling of togetherness was vividly demonstrated for people in my own congregation one Friday night when our guest speaker was the charismatic Bishop Fulton Sheen who, in his own way, did much to make the American people aware of their commonalty. Before Pope John, Catholics were not permitted into houses of worship other than their own—yet here was a Bishop not only in a synagogue but serving as the guest preacher at a Sabbath service!

Bishop Sheen began his discourse with these meaningful words: "I am glad to be here in this Jewish temple to tell my friends of the Jewish faith how sorry I am that your people and mine have been separated over the course of these centuries by a lovers' quarrel."

A lovers' quarrel! If the separation of Christians and Jews was a protracted family misunderstanding, then young people on campuses, in shops, and in offices could no longer withstand the allurements of romantic attraction because of diverse belief. Such was the unconscious reaction of many to the unification of the ecumenical era.

The result was a rash of intermarriages, and a rush to ministers to solemnize them. Ministers, priests, and rabbis scarcely knew how to cope with the new demands. Christian clergymen were not quite as upset as Jewish ones, because the former had always been willing to provide a Christian ceremony to a mixed pair, in the hope that the non-Christian would then convert. However, the Jews had no missionary program; we did not proselytize, and we had always abstained from officiating at mixed marriages. Actually, of course, we had watched thousands of our people ignore us completely when they decided to marry out of the faith. They would go off to churches or to magistrates' courts and would thereafter forget their Jewishness.

Ecumenism also bore another fruit which gradually impinged on us. With the lowering of barriers between religions there grew an appreciation for Judaism.

Movies, books, magazine feature articles, plays, and television programs suddenly began to glorify Judaism. The best-seller lists included many treatments of Judaism. Events in the State of Israel put Jews on front pages, and books and articles dealt with the Jewish people and the Jewish faith. Hollywood and Broadway had always included a large segment of Jews, but they had previously been self-conscious and timid about their identification. Now it was "in" to be Jewish.

The two most glamorous actresses of their age turned Jewish, and this engendered a thousand talk show discussions about Jewishness. We have had Presidents named Monroe and Taylor, but their impact on the mores of their times was small compared with the impact produced by Marilyn Monroe and Elizabeth Taylor, the two most glamorous and clamorous beauties of our era. The rabbi who gave instructions to Marilyn was asked how long the period of training would be and he answered, "As long as possible." One of his parishioners scolded him for not staging her conversion in the Yale Bowl, at a dollar a head, and thus wipe out the large deficit under which his New Haven temple was groaning.

Judaism abruptly penetrated not only books on theology and articles in serious literary journals but also was featured in movie magazines whose readers were given glow-by-glow descriptions of the way their female idols embraced the new faith. Never before had religion reached such a large segment of our populace in such an effective fashion. If Marilyn and Liz could have rabbis tie their marital knots, why couldn't they do likewise?

And their fans—and many more—gravitated to our studies. They asked us to give them a Jewish ceremony. We were nonplussed. We didn't have what they wanted. The Jewish marriage ritual is designed for two people who accept the teachings of Moses! It didn't seem suitable for a couple that was not within the Jewish fold.

The reaction of rabbis was one of bewilderment. On one hand, we wanted to keep these young people, and we were delighted that they wanted to be united in a Jewish ceremony. On the other hand, we didn't know how to satisfy their demands. And "on the third hand," we couldn't urge the non-Jewish partner to become Jewish because Judaism does not have a program for the recruitment of gentiles. There is an even greater difficulty here: traditional Judaism, in the eyes of some interpreters, put a tabu on conversions which took place for matrimonial reasons. Marriage was not regarded a serious enough motive for entrance into Judaism. If one wanted to turn Jewish, it should be because of the attractions of its precepts, not of its adherents. This is a classic teaching in the Hebrew tradition.

Another oddity in the new rabbi-ward surge of affianced couples was their desire for a "lot of religion" in their ceremony. Previously, couples would sometimes ask the rabbi, "Don't make it too religious," or "Please keep out the Hebrew." That was not an uncommon request even when both partners were Jewish. Now, the couples not only wanted a rabbi with a completely Jewish ritual, but they wanted more religion and they often wanted two ministers to join them together. Two ministers, that is, of different faiths. Some wanted three clergymen—Catholic, Protestant, *and* Jewish—because they had relatives of each faith.

This banging on the church and synagogue doors produced great changes in some dioceses and temples. The pre-Vatican Council policies of the Roman Catholic Church were strict. If a member of the church intermarried, the outsider had to sign a paper committing the children to Catholicism. The non-Catholic partner, if he or she adhered to non-Catholicism, had to stand "behind the rail." Efforts were made to convert the non-Catholic.

In counselling sessions, the Catholic drawn to a person of
another faith was admonished that their partner would be
denied the joys of afterlife in the company of the devout.
Indeed, there was some doubt as to whether a Catholic
who intermarried would still be eligible for the joys of the
other world. Written permission was needed for an irreg-
ular espousal. Priests were reluctant to become involved
in intermarriages. When they did acquiesce, the priests
insisted on a completely trinitarian ceremony. Indeed,
there was no provision in most priests' manuals for any
other kind of ceremony.

To a great extent, this has now changed. The changes
in Catholic liturgy are generally amazing. Whereas at one
time it was impossible to insert an English word into the
Latin litany, Latin has now been virtually banished. On a
radio program which I do with a priest and a Protestant
minister, we interviewed a young Catholic priest. I asked
him whether he had ever done a mass in Latin, and he
said no. He was next asked whether he *could* do a Latin
mass, and astoundingly the answer was again no.

In dozens of weddings which I have performed in
tandem with Roman Catholic and Protestant ministers,
the deference on the part of my Christian colleagues to
the sensitivities of their Jewish partner has been incredible.
Many of them have so modified their procedures that
there is no mention of the trinity or of Jesus. In the
manuals published for the benefit of Roman Catholic
priests, there is now a marriage service designed for a
mixed couple. In that service there is not a Christological

trace, so far have the Christian groups leaned over backwards to spare the feelings of Jewish partners.

Within the Jewish faith, we rabbis had to do extensive soul-searching before some of us agreed to take part in a marriage "mix." Mixed couples originally got a universal negative response from all rabbis. The reasoning is understandable; we told applying couples that we did not have what they wanted: a ritual for a Jew and a non-Jew. All we had was a ceremony for two people within the Jewish fold. We advised couples to have a civil ceremony. When we were told that Christian ministers were willing to be involved and were asked why we rabbis should be less tolerant than our Christian counterparts, we fell back on the explanation that we do not solicit recruits to our faith the way Christians do. We maintained our opposition to the very idea of solemnizing a union betwen a Jew and a non-Jew.

Gradually, we began to have second thoughts; we began to realize that we were in a new era.

Whereas in the past couples who intermarried did so because of a dearth of religious feeling, we discovered that many of these new couples earnestly wanted a religious presence at their wedding—and often a double one.

We realized that if, at the crucial juncture of their marriage, we were to turn our backs on them they might permanently turn their backs on us.

My wife put it very succinctly when she said to me, "If you can save one family or one person for Judaism by consenting to take part in a wedding, you must do so."

What could be the rationale for so marked a deviation from earlier norms? How could one justify such a change? Oddly enough, there is a traditional buttress for what some rabbis now do. To be sure, our reasoning is strongly contested and vigorously opposed by those who not only disagree with us but also assail us for our "heresy." However, in the Talmud we read somewhere that in determining a proper policy one must not entirely rely on a rabbinical panel, although new laws are sometimes fashioned by such a body. It is not always helpful to rely only on previous rulings by rabbinical courts, although that should frequently be done. Biblical citations and rabbinical precedents may indeed yield guidance (just as earlier decrees by the Supreme Court can aid contemporary jurists in deciding what is Constitutional). The Talmudical passage referred to above is one in which a rabbinical authority asserts that in some cases one can learn what Judaism calls for by going into the community and seeing "what the people do."

And the people were ahead of the rabbis in the matter of intermarriage. They experienced a surge of interest in Judaism; they wanted a Jewish "presence" at their marriages. In many instances they wanted more: they wanted two religious officiants.

When requests began to mount for rabbis to join Christian ministers in performing marriages, we were scandalized. How can you have a ceremony in which allegiance to Christianity and dedication to Judaism are meshed? It was outrageous, it was unthinkable.

However, some of us continued to ponder the matter.

The essence of the Jewish ceremony is a declaration on the part of the bridegroom that he consecrates himself as a husband to the bride "according to the law of Moses and Israel" (Israel meaning the Jewish people, not that state in the Middle East).

My thought led me to the conviction that a non-Jew *could* make such a declaration. Christianity has not repudiated the outlook of Moses and Judaism with respect to family life. Both Judaism and Christianity subscribe to wholesomeness, holiness, and devotion within the home. There are many Jewish couples who are no more meticulous than non-Jews in their adherence to Jewish practice; yet there would be no hesitancy in providing them with a Jewish ceremony. Why deny that privilege to a non-Jew who is asking for a rabbi's blessing?

True, there is a long history of Jewish frowning on marriages with outsiders. In the Bible, specific bans on marriage with certain peoples are laid down. In the Book of Ezra, as we have pointed out, the zealous scribe is actually said to have forced Jewish husbands to separate themselves from their non-Jewish wives.

There is also a counter-tradition which is hospitable to the idea of Jews marrying out, especially if the non-Jewish partners displayed deference to the Jewish idea of monotheism. Moses himself intermarried. So did Joseph before him, and Esther after him. Even though the Bible proscribes the Edomites as marriage partners, the Book of Ruth features an Edomite, Ruth herself, who not only marries a Jew, Boaz, but also becomes the progenitress of David, and therefore of the hoped-for messiah. With respect to the foreign wives banished by Ezra, their fault lay not in their origin but in their idolatrous propensities.

In short, the ban against non-Jewish marriage partners was aimed at pagans or idolaters. Christians, or persons of Christian birth who were not zealous in their trinitarian practices, were, in our eyes, not to be regarded as pagans. Therefore, we told ourselves, they are not in the category of those forbidden as mates for Jews. They could, in good conscience, make the declaration that they would live in keeping with the laws of Moses and in conformity with the family standards of the Jewish faith.

We even made a distinction between Christians married by a rabbi and Jews married by a Christian minister whose rites were trinitarian.

We reasoned that everything that is in Judaism is also in Christianity. Christianity is Judaism plus the trinitarian idea. Not everything that is in Christianity is to be found in Judaism, for the latter, as explained above, does not subscribe to the apotheosis of Jesus or to many other dogmas under the Cross. This explains why Christians are usually not offended by what happens in a synagogue or during a Jewish ceremony, and why Jews feel out of place in a church or feel uncomfortable during a trinitarian ceremony.

I am delighted to salute the Christian ministers with whom I have been allied in the conduct of wedding rites for their understanding, their kindness, and their care during the course of these proceedings.

Now how does one go about presiding at the union of

a Jew and a non-Jew? Painfully and slowly, I arrived at a course of action. The same concern was felt by dozens of other rabbis who were taking the same steps towards some solution of this difficult problem.

No two rabbis adopted the same method. Rabbis are notoriously independent and cannot be straightjacketed. It is true that the general profile of a Jewish marriage ceremony is substantially the same for all Jewish clergymen, but variations are possible and permissible, and this latitude is fully taken advantage of by professional practitioners.

Some rabbis decided that they would be part of an intermarriage if they could get certain provisos agreed upon by the parties concerned. Some insist that at some future time the non-Jew should be converted. Some demand that any children of the marriage be raised as Jews. Some stipulate that a course of instruction should precede the marriage even if the gentile does not change religions. One rabbi devised a ceremony of his own in which the couple are given certain statements to make, so that the rabbi becomes more of a witness to an arrangement rather than an officiant. The late Dr. Samuel Baron concocted a long, original ceremony, replete with references to both Judaism and Christianity. That text was widely used by Dr. Baron and Christian colleagues of his who became something of a marrying team in the Greater New York area.

Some rabbis limited their conduct of intermarriages to their own members. Others restricted their activities in this regard to their own community. Some refused to permit an intermarriage to take place in the synagogue sanctuary. Most rabbis refused to step into a church for the purpose of participating in a marriage ceremony.

Almost all of the rabbis refused to violate the strict rule against performing a marriage on the Sabbath or on any of the Jewish festivals equivalent to the Sabbath. One exception to that last rule was a rabbi, ironically with an Orthodox background, who cited a traditional Jewish practice in which wedding blessings are recited on the Sabbath, even though the actual knot-tying may not occur then. He extenuated his participation in Sabbath unions by stating that all he did was to recite those blessings.

Having convinced myself that the non-Jew who comes to me is saying in effect that he wants to be guided by Jewish ideals even if he does not formally transfer his faith to Judaism, I give my couples a ceremony which is essentially traditional. Often the rites I offer to a mixed couple are more Orthodox than those I give to an all-Jewish couple who are Reform. The request for traditionalist elements frequently emanates from the non-Jewish family!

It is my contention that any ritual which is Jewish is actually *not* Jewish. By this I mean that the significance of any Jewish practice has universal application. Indeed, I feel that Judaism itself is the ideal faith for an ideal society. Whatever has become sanctified in Jewish history transcends the Jewish people alone.

Let me see if I can explain this paradox. The holiest day of the Jewish religious calendar is Yom Kippur, the Day of Atonement, the climactic event of the ten-day period of repentance often termed the Jewish High Holy Days. "High" is really a loan from Christianity. The Ten Days are an interval of introspection and admittance of past failures and faults, an appeal to God for forgiveness for our derelictions, and a plea to God for the strength to grant forgiveness to those who have hurt us.

Even marginal Jews are stirred to come to the synagogue on the High Holy Days, which are marked by worship services at the beginning of the ten-day skein and by gatherings on the tenth day, the aforementioned Day of Atonement. Jews who do not attend worship services throughout the year gravitate back to the synagogue then in what I term "station identification."

Now what is there about this sacred Jewish day that is Jewish? Its background is, of course, Hebraic, but is there anything about the Day of Atonement which limits its call to the Jews? Its call is for confession of our shortcomings. The actual procedure is to fast, to abstain from food, to suffer a bit as a reminder of the suffering we have visited upon others. The prescribed prayers for this observance deal with our weaknesses as human beings, our proneness to sin, our desecration of that which is godly within us. That's the bad news. The good news is that the Almighty has given us the power to improve, to rise above our present moral level to a higher stage of daily living. Now there's nothing specifically, distinctively Jewish about that: it applies to all people. It is human, not particularistic. No wonder a Christian minister once recommended that the churches join the synagogues in observing Yom Kippur!

What is true of Yom Kippur is true of every Jewish observance.

At the wedding ceremonies I conduct, I briefly dwell on the significance of every segment of the rite and make all on hand feel that the teachings of Judaism are significant for all.

The ceremony includes a series of blessings, originally seven in number, all of which begin, as every Jewish blessing does, with three little words: "*Baruch attah adoshem.*" After pronouncing them, I explain that these three words, often translated as "Praised be Thou, O God," actually mean "Thanks to God," and I urge upon the couple an everlasting attitude of gratitude to Him for all the favors they have received in their lifetime and plead with the couple to comport themselves so that their partners will echo these three words frequently.

The Jewish ceremony includes the sipping of wine. I point out that the wine is symbolic. As it is sweet, so the lives of the bride and groom have been sweetened by family affection. I offer the hope that the chain reaction of sweet family affection, exemplified by the wine, will continue.

The wedding rings are bright; this, I indicate, is an augury of the need to add brightness to each other's life.

The rings are round. This should be a reminder that the couple is now included in a large circle of affinity. I say that marriage involves a widening of the circle of affection. The wedding bands also symbolize the fact that all of mankind is a "family circle," and should prompt the couple to do what they can to help the cause of universal brotherhood.

When the groom recites the statement, "I consecrate myself to you as your husband in accordance with the teachings of the faith of Israel" (my phraseology), I comment that the Jewish faith calls upon the marriage partners to be constant and faithful to one another and to create a home which will brim with affection.

One prayer is a reminder that the Hebrew word for marriage is *Kiddushin*, which does not actually translate as marriage but rather as sanctification, underscoring the need for the partners to look upon one another and their goal in life as something sacred.

The wedding canopy (Hebrew: *chuppah*) is cited as a symbol of "the intimacies and the responsibilities of that sacred enclosure which we call the home."

The ceremony ends with the groom stamping on a glass. Before that happens I indicate that the glass recalls the ancient sanctuary, one wall of which still stands in Jerusalem. Ever since it was destroyed, I state, every sensitive person in the Judeo-Christian family has been mandated to rebuild it.

I add, "We are not called upon necessarily to restore the edifice itself, but we are obligated to build a life which will reflect the principles that emanated from that shrine: the belief that all mankind is one family, that every human being is sacred, that man can break out of strife and misunderstanding into the bright sunlight of harmony and peace, that we can achieve the triumph of the decent over the merely recent." I furthermore remind the couple that marriage is as fragile as glass and that stamping on the glass dramatizes the need to avoid impulsiveness and tempestuousness.

All of these lessons are Jewish, but none of them is exclusively Jewish. The mixed audiences who absorb this exposition receive an orientation about some of the most important Jewish values. The couple realizes that marriage has spiritual implications. They also get an unexpected insight into the outlook of Judaism. Of course, they also receive this from the pre-nuptial interviews and from the reading matter about Judaism I give to all couples.

As a result, many non-Jews who undergo this marriage ceremony decide, on their own, to become Jewish. The influx of gentiles into Judaism is one of the most fascinating stories *never* told.

The decision by some rabbis to solemnize mixed marriages triggered a convulsion (and revulsion) within Jewish organizational life. The national association of liberal rabbis, known as the Central Conference of American Rabbis, underwent a considerable upheaval over the matter. The Conference had several times passed resolutions urging its members to discourage intermarriage. When the incidence of rabbi-conducted mixed marriage began to increase, the then leadership of the Conference urged the adoption of more stringent measures. For two years the matter was studied, debated, and argued. Finally, the issue came to a vote, and by a 60-40 majority the Conference officially stated that it deplored the practice of those rabbis who performed intermarriages.

What astonished observers was not that the majority took this action, but that the majority was so small. Tacked onto the resolution was a statement that those who did not participate in mixed marriages respected the position of those who did so.

Many rabbis were angry not so much over the deviation from the long-standing practice of abstaining from any role in intermarriage but over the fact that colleagues of theirs would come to their area from other parts of the country in order to officiate. A rabbi would be asked by a member of his congregation to provide a Jewish wedding ceremony. He would refuse. Then the family would hear that another rabbi, in another region, was available, and would "import" him. This is a transgression of professional ethics, and is, of course, resented by the local rabbi—just as your doctor or lawyer would take umbrage at your switching to others without giving him the courtesy of notification. The "intermarriers" in Reform ranks acknowledged the validity of this stricture, and most of us will not minister to the parishioner of another rabbi without proper clearance.

Still, the disclosure that some 40 percent of the American Reform rabbinate no longer regarded furnishing a mixed couple with a Jewish ceremony as shocking did evoke astonishment. The Conservative rabbinate abstains from this practice, although a number of its practitioners do officiate at such weddings. One of them was expelled from the ranks of the official group, the Rabbinical Assembly of America, not because of his marrying practices, but because he ignored a call from the group to present himself before a hearing.

The Orthodox rabbis, as can be understood, are highly indignant over this new development. Still, the matter has given them problems. Their parishioners are not immune from romantic crossovers and frequently they are asked to give a mixed couple a Jewish ceremony. Naturally, they demur. However, when they are asked to do so by influential families in the synagogue, they are often placed in a dilemma. What to do? Some urge the conversion of the non-Jew, even though that isn't quite the "kosher" thing to do. Others cling to their convictions and, if all else fails, abstain from involvement even if it means the alienation of the family and their resignation from the synagogue. Some clandestinely refer the family to a Reform colleague to do what the Orthodox rabbi believes that Jewish law (known as *halacha*) forbids him to do.

Indeed, one Reform "intermarrier" says that he began his new practice as the result of a plea from an Orthodox rabbi whose own daughter insisted on "marrying out." The rabbi called his liberal colleague and said, in effect: "I can't officiate at my daughter's marriage because her fiance isn't Jewish. She says that if she isn't married Jewishly she will walk out of my life. I want a chance to have Jewish grandchildren so I beg you to perform this wedding."

I have performed weddings for the offspring of traditional rabbis and for the children of officials of Orthodox synagogues. In almost every case, the parents have thanked me profusely for what I did, declaring that the Jewish ceremony I provided gave the families a "fighting chance" to keep the young couple involved within the ambiance of Jewish life.

The novelty of rabbis' offering a Jewish ceremony to "mixes" also precipitated a much-publicized controversy within the ranks of the New York Board of Rabbis, a body containing clergymen from all three of the Jewish groups.

In an outburst of zeal, the leadership of the Board (or a segment of it) decided to move against rabbis who participated in intermarriages. A resolution was promulgated expelling them from the Board. The proposal was enthusiastically endorsed by the traditionalists but was opposed, of course, by many of the liberals and also by some of the Conservative rabbis who, although they did not approve of solemnizing mixed marriages, felt that it would be a bad precedent for the Board to interfere in the practices of its members.

The controversy led to a full-fledged debate. There was no time for a vote. Then the president of the Board, a Conservative rabbi, unexpectedly announced that the vote would be held on a nearby Friday. It was summer, and many rabbis were on vacation. The Orthodox faithful were rallied by telephone to attend the meeting. Many came who had never before appeared at a Board meeting. The deliberations wore on and some had to leave to prepare for Sabbath eve services. The president permitted them to cast their vote before the discussion was concluded. Ultimately, the vote was taken and the intermarriers were expelled.

The resolution called for the expulsion of the intermarriers and also for those who "referred" families to the offenders; that part of the action has not been enforced.

In some quarters the Board came under fire for its hasty action, and murmurs were heard to the effect that it would be rescinded at a later date. In the meantime, the ultra-Orthodox began agitating for the resignation of all traditionalists from the Board on the grounds that many of the Board members violate other halachic injunctions having to do with the remarriage of divorcees without a Jewish writ or the espousal of descendants of the priestly caste to forbidden partners: widows, divorced women, etc.

The matter even had repercussions in Israel, where the Orthodox political party demanded that the government stop granting Jewish identification cards to people who became converts to Judaism via procedures not consistent with Orthodox rules. Most Reform rabbis, however, respectfully differ with their Orthodox colleagues who practice what we call "biological Judaism," that is, the insistence that one of the major criteria of a person's Jewishness is to have had a Jewish mother. To many Reform rabbis, nurture is more important than nature.

Back in the U.S., the demand for a Jewish ceremony for mixed couples has continued unabated. So persistent is this demand that there has, lamentably, arisen a cluster of free-lance rabbis and cantors who are commercializing the enterprise. Cantors are permitted to function as marriers, and most of them are kosher. A small fringe, however, is less so, and this is also true of some "rabbis" whose ordinations are suspect. In fact, some of us intermarriers have been lumped with this coterie and we are often accused of doing what we do for monetary reasons. Occasionally when someone asks me, "What is your fee?" and I give my standard response, "Nothing," there's a gasp of incredulity. Let me add that most people do offer an honorarium, but that my greatest reward is the satisfaction of being of service and perhaps assuring the survival of my faith.

The eagerness of many couples for a Jewish blessing for their nuptials is spectacular.

Take, for example, the Bob Hope family. One of Mr. Hope's daughters was to be married to the son of a prominent Augusta, Georgia, physician.

The ceremony was set for a Catholic church in Hollywood. The Hopes wanted the ceremony to include a rabbinic touch, since the Jewish family belonged to the Reform temple in their home city. The rabbi there is the famed Dr. Norman Goldburg, whose books describing the chaplaincy in which he served during World War II have made him a national favorite.

Bob and Mrs. Hope transported Rabbi and Mrs. Goldburg across the continent so that a Hebrew blessing would be pronounced over the couple.

In my own case, families have "shlepped" me long distances so that the Jewish moment in the weddings would be assured. In one instance, the family secured for me a small, private plane, complete, of course, with pilot and co-pilot, which whisked me into Vermont for a wedding. At the small airport a car was waiting. When we landed, we rode off into the snowy landscape to the place where the wedding took place. After my brief stint, my drivers drove me back to the airport and soon I was flying over

New England. Back to White Plains I came and then drove off in my car to another wedding.

During the course of one summer, I was "imported" to Vancouver, British Columbia, for a wedding and then to San Juan, Puerto Rico, for another one.

In Vancouver I united a Jewish doctor to a Congregationalist medical student. The ceremony was in the home of the bride. The wedding party included guests from India, from Japan, from Scotland and elsewhere. Most of them had never met a rabbi before, let alone attended a Jewish marriage rite.

In Santurce, a suburb of San Juan, I helped unite a Jewish bride and a Roman Catholic bridegroom. The Roman Catholics were made aware for the first time that the parents of Jesus were linked by the same rituals that are now used in Jewish weddings.

Another long-distance wedding I performed was in Port au Prince, Haiti, where I had gone to conduct a Bar Mitzvah for the son of a cousin of mine. When two families whose children were being wed learned of my presence there, they asked me to give "Jewish validation" to the marriage of their progeny. On hand, in an elegant home, were about a hundred guests, of all faiths and hues.

On a portable organ, my wife played the wedding music. Those on hand were intrigued by the Hebrew blessings and the charge which I gave the couple. There followed, during the reception, a seminar on Judaism.

Years ago Jewish intermarriers would not have bothered to secure a rabbi for their nuptials. And non-Jewish families would have scorned the idea of introducing a Jewish note to the proceedings even if one partner was Hebraic.

But it is a sign of the times that nowadays both the Jewish and Christian families are avid in their desire for rabbinical participation. The degree of their avidity is attested to by the few examples I have here cited.

How to Make
Intermarriages Work

Despite the complexities involved, many intermarriages are successful.

In an era of multitudinous divorces and casual coupling without benefit of clergy, marriages do thrive. The institution of marriage remains one of the staples of our society.

As indicated earlier, the possibilities of a break-up are more numerous in the case of marital crossovers. However, despite the pitfalls, many people marry and "live happily ever afterwards." Interfaith and even interracial unions are numerous among the successful marriages.

The success of an intermarriage is like the success of an intramarriage; it depends on a continuous effort on the part of the pair to sustain the high tide of romance.

Sometimes, the challenge to the harmony of a union evokes from husband and wife special efforts and ingenuity which provide a tingle which, in turn, enhances the marriage.

If you have something to live for, chances are that you will put forth greater effort. An intermarried couple has something to live for: not only their own mutual happiness, but also the proof that the alarmists were wrong all the time.

This extra purpose has sometimes produced an added zest in the determination of intermarried couples to defy the odds.

One correspondent who wrote to me about his desire to marry out of his faith said that his family was constantly bothering him with the question, "What will your children be?"

He wrote, "I'm interested in Betty and myself, not in future children." The young man was right: if a husband and wife can attain a measure of felicity, their chances of managing the lives of their children will be considerably easier.

In deciding whom to marry, and in determining what religious course to follow, the couple should not give priority to the destiny of their offspring, if any. They must regard their own situation as the essential criterion.

It happens that the woods—and the cities—are full of intermarriages. Descendants of President Tyler and Supreme Court Justice Hughes are married to Jews. Rockefellers and Wasps and members of the Social Register are married to Jewish partners.

Not long ago a newspaper social item informed us that a rabbi officiated at the wedding of a Brodsky to the great-granddaughter of the President of Uruguay.

Varied though the backgrounds of many of these couples are, they have managed to synchronize their lives successfully.

So, if a couple is contemplating a mixed marriage, one

course it could follow is to consult with those who have weathered the potential storms and ask them how they did it.

Any important project merits preparation. Marriage itself is something which should prompt one to research and investigation. Bookstores are full of marriage manuals and advice to the lovelorn. If marriage as such is worthy of advanced study, then an intermarriage certainly warrants it.

A couple might ask around and learn the names of those who are involved in this situation. I have found that most of them are eager to talk, to dispense the fruit of their experiences. Young people could sit down and talk at length with successful intermarrieds, if there is such a term, and quiz them penetratingly on how they managed, how they dealt with their families, how they live religiously, how they cope with the vicissitudes of their condition. Chances are that an engaged pair who embarked upon this kind of survey would greatly benefit from it.

The couple might in all probability not only learn what steps are advisable, but also what to avoid. The research project could, of course, include queries about the problem of children.

The premarital exploration should also include visits to clergymen. To us in the ministry, marriage, and now intermarriage, are what apples and oranges are to the grocer, and our stock of data is available to all inquirers.

Just as there is no formula that can guarantee a smooth marriage, there is no panacea for a problem-free mixed union.

A rule of thumb might be that where one partner has stronger religious feelings it would be advisable for the other one to adopt the other faith. If a devout Christian, who takes his religion earnestly, is wed to a lukewarm Jew, Christianity might be the best outlook to accept. It may seem odd for a rabbi to suggest that Jews go Christian, but family stability is more important to me than Jewish numbers. When the Jewish partner is more devout, the non-Jew would be well-advised to "go Jewish."

Such decisions have proved salutary in many cases. The Jewish partner thinks little of his own ancestral faith; he or she is perfectly willing to make the transfer for the sake of family unity. Everyone reading this knows of instances where this has proved a satisfactory solution.

Then there are cases where the couple is actually able to perform the feat of incorporating two religions in one household. The father, say, stays Jewish, patronizes the synagogue, while the Christian mother remains loyal to her church.

This kind of balancing act becomes quite precarious if children are born. However, in some cases it is done with amazing dexterity. There is an old chestnut about the young man who says to his fiancee, "I must tell you that I'm anemic."

"Well," she replies, "that's OK. You go to your church and I'll go to mine."

In an intriguing article in *The New York Times*, the head of that newspaper's Athens bureau, a Jew named Mr. Roberts, tells how he and his wife, who was brought

up in a convent, took their two little children on a tour of
Israel. In the course of the narrative, Mr. Roberts tells
about the way they traveled through the Holy Land with
a Bible as a Baedeker, flitting from Jewish to Christian to
Moslem holy places, and apparently giving their children
an appreciation of the traditions of each of the faiths. Mr.
Roberts describes the mutual appreciation he and his wife
displayed for each other's religious background and how
their children were receiving a kind of a synthetic faith,
to the extent that in Greece, one of them said that there
were three gods: "God, Jesus, and Zeus."

At the end of the tour through Israel, the 6-year-old
Roberts' child tossed a puzzle at his mother: "Mom, what
does a Jew and a Christian make?" The answer: "A me."

Many a "me" has grown up in a family where both
Judaism and Christianity were practiced. Although seemingly awkward, this process may result in a realization of
the similarities of the two religions. The rising call for
wedding services with two ministers of different faiths
reflects a new understanding of the essential affinity of the
two Bible-born faiths. Pat Boone put it differently when
he said, "There are really four kinds of Jews: Orthodox,
Conservative, Reform, and Christian."

The new era to which I allude has given rise to a multi-
tude of conversions to Judaism by former Christians. As
I have said before, this is one of the greatest stories never
told. It is an astonishing phenomenon, considering that
Jews are still subject to disabilities. The normal trend
would be to have those in the minority opt to escape the

restrictions of their status and to move upward to a status where there is freedom from handicaps. Conversions to Christianity still outnumber those to Judaism by far.

The reversing of the usual tendency reflects the strong appeal of Judaism, especially to many sensitive Christians.

Let me repeat that modern Jews do not proselytize. Yes, it is true that since the founding of the independent state of Israel small organizations calling for the recruitment of Christians have arisen in the Jewish body politic. These groups have urged the enlargement of their efforts. Judaism, they say, is too fine a commodity for Jews to keep it to themselves. It should be shared.

Let it also be stated that there was a time when Jews did ardently proselytize. The New Testament contains a description of those Pharisees who would cross heaven and earth to sign up a new Jew. The signing up went on apace at the turn of the millennium. Shortly after the birth of Christianity, a vigorous rivalry ensued between Jews and the Paulinians and the Judaizers did very well indeed. They lined up relatives of the crucially important imperial family; they campaigned up and down the avenues of Rome and other communities; they competed with the zealots of the Christian communes to win the allegiance of the "pagans"—but they lost out. What made the Jewish drive extremely difficult were the requirements of circumcision and lengthy instruction for those who wanted to become Jewish. The Christians abolished these rather cumbersome prerequisites. The Christians also traded heavily upon the "pie in the sky" doctrine, giving their prospects the impression that the next world was full of glittering rewards for those who went Christian.

After their success in capturing the imperial Roman throne, which meant that they were now the religious style-setters for what was then the entire Western world, the Christians turned upon the Jews.

For centuries, the Christians importuned and often compelled the Jews to relinquish their faith. The dogged and brutal proselytizing methods of the Christians soured the Jews on missionaries. In modern times as well, the Jew looked upon those seeking to beguile him to give up his faith in favor of the infant Jesus with great distaste. Hence, the idea of soliciting people to change religions is now held in disfavor by the Jews.

This negative attitude towards solicitation was reinforced by a Talmudical dictum that a person who wants to become Jewish for the purposes of matrimony was to be rebuffed. Conversion was deemed much too important a step to be predicated on marriage alone. If one wanted to become Jewish it should be for reasons of conviction and not for reasons of marriage.

Despite this background, the recent rush to Judaism precisely because of marriage has been brisk.

When I interview Christians who decide to embrace Judaism in order to embrace a Jewish spouse, I find that they often feel a sense of relief in their new religion.

The relief is occasioned, they tell me, by the reasonableness of the Jewish faith and outlook. Judaism lacks some of the dogmas which Christians are expected to accept.

To be Christian and seriously so, one has to believe that Mary was born in a certain way. One must accept the recondite trinitarian concept, which is difficult enough to explain—let alone understand. One must subscribe to the article of faith about the miraculous manner in which Jesus was conceived, with its unconscious corollary that there is something unclean about normal sexual relations. One must exalt Jesus because of his skill in the performance of miracles. The miracles are usually some interference in the regular processes of nature. A devout Christian denigrates this world in favor of the glories of a putative other one. A genuine follower of Jesus must subscribe to the notion of "original sin," which means that all men are tainted because of what happened in Eden. The Christian is called upon to believe that the voluntary sacrifice of Jesus atones for that Garden of Eden default. If you take Christianity seriously, you must also give credence to the resurrection of Jesus three days after his demise.

All of these beliefs can make a person gentle, compassionate, and sensitive; they can render him a "true Christian." However, they are difficult to accept. As a result, there are legions of fallen-away Christians who are only nominally religious, and who either ignore or give little attention to these theological dicta.

In Judaism, on the other hand, one is not expected to subscribe to arcane mysteries. You can be a Jew and a subscriber to the ethics of Moses without even believing that there ever was a Moses. If the existence of Jesus (about whom we know nothing except from the New Testament) were disproved, Christianity might totter. In

Judaism it is not the historical existence of Moses which is essential; it is the ideas ascribed to Moses which form the basis of the faith.

True, the Jewish "Bible" also recounts stories of supernatural events. However, you can be kosher and cast a skeptical eye on the actuality of those events, since the basis of Judaism is a cluster of ideals which should inspire our behavior, not subscription to the actuality of any happenings. In Reform Judaism, especially, many of the Biblical stories are deemed allegorical rather than actual. As for difficult-to-swallow dogmas, there are very few indeed, although difficult-to-follow ideals abound.

All of which calls to mind a delightful tale about a Christian minister and a rabbi on a sight-seeing tour of Israel. As the tour guide described the events associated with the various holy places, Jewish and Christian, they both nodded their heads, recalling the appropriate Scriptural passages. Finally, the rabbi said to his Christian counterpart: "All of those stories about Jesus, you don't believe them, do you?" To which the cleric replied: "What about all the stories in the Old Testament, the splitting of the Red Sea, Elijah flying off into air, etc.?" Retorted the rabbi: "Don't you know the difference between fact and fiction?"

The one difficult-to-believe Jewish idea that the devout are called upon to accept is that there *is* a God. The nature of God and His appearance are subject to dispute and there are legitimate differences of viewpoint concerning these matters in Hebraic lore. However, a case for the existence of God can be made on the basis of scientific induction rather than dogmatic dictate. If everything in the world reflects a maker and a purpose, isn't it logical to believe that the world itself possesses those characteristics? Could all of the symmetries and orderliness in the universe be the product of happenstance and chance? Don't they rather point to some Brain who conceived of it all?

Judaism also teaches that the source and force behind the world urges goodness upon us. We believe that the conscience is God's mark inside of every person. Our conscience nudges us individually, and society collectively, to improve the moral caliber of our conduct.

To fortify this upward tug, the Jewish faith is filled with observances and rituals designed to enhance the quality of life.

There are three festivals, originally agricultural, which underscore important themes. The Spring Festival of Passover glorifies the idea of freedom and calls upon all to re-live the adventures of those who were in the land of bondage and later journeyed to the land of promise. Pentecost (*Shavuot*, in Hebrew), fifty days later, celebrates the giving of the Ten Commandments. Whether they were announced on Sinai or transmitted through sensitive sages, the Commandments are the way to a finer world. The third major festival, in the autumn, is mankind's first Holiday of Thanksgiving. Called Tabernacles (Hebrew: *Sukkot*), it reminds us of the frail abodes which the first freedom fighters occupied in the desert for forty years and induces an attitude of appreciation to the Divine Conscience Who implanted within the hearts of human beings the desire for liberty, even when that prize entails a heavy price of suffering and hardship.

The Jewish calendar has been termed the catechism of the Jewish faith. At the beginning of the spiritual (not the secular) year, there is a ten-day period of public confession and private acknowledgment of one's faults and failings. Known as the High Holy Day period, the period of observance begins on *Rosh Hashanah* (the New Year) with the blast of the ram's horn, which awakens the worshipper from moral slothfulness, and reaches its culmination ten days later with *Yom Kippur* (Day of Atonement) which is given over to fasting to remind us of the discomfort we have caused others, our quest for forgiveness from God for our derelictions, and our quest for strength to grant forgiveness to those who have wronged us.

To one reared in the Christian faith, acceptance of the insights underlying these holidays does not involve an emotional or ideological wrench. This is not true of a Jew asked to make Jesus his savior and to give intellectual acceptance to the complex dogmas surrounding the Christian faith.

Nor do the Jewish High Holy Days present mental difficulties for one brought up in a Christian household. The appeal of the Holy Days is not limited to any one group. The ram's horn sounds for all sensitive people who rejoice that they have been so constituted that they can improve. The theme of the Holy Days is one which can win universal acceptance. You don't have to be born Jewish to appreciate the message or its implications in terms of behavior.

Some years ago a Christian clergyman called upon his

fellow-communicants to join the Jews in observing the High Holy Days. He pointed out that there was nothing exclusively Jewish about the penitential season and that both Judaism and Christianity are rooted in the same traditions which call upon people to confess their shortcomings and strive to lead a life acceptable to the God that both groups extol.

Within the context of an intermarriage, the partner who was originally Christian can readily shift ideological gears and be comfortable within the Jewish tradition. This is not merely a theory. In every synagogue in the country there are converts from Christianity who have taken their place easily in synagogue pews. Some of them have even become congregational leaders.

I was once associated with the national headquarters of the Reform Jewish movement. In my capacity as public relations director for that movement I came into contact with leaders of temples throughout the country. A goodly number of them were converts from Christianity. Among the women who have leading posts in the Sisterhoods of the nation's Reform temples converts are also to be found. They are numbered among those who sit on the national executive board of the central body, which is known as the Union of American Hebrew Congregations. Beyond that, we have some rabbis who started out as non-Jews, and also a quorum of rabbis' wives, not to mention several cantors (those who provide liturgical music at worship gatherings).

In the City of New York so many couples are mixed that a Reform rabbi created a congregation designed to serve them. Rabbi Roy Rosenberg has disproved the assertion that there is nothing new under the sun. His congregation is based upon the thesis that most of the couples subscribe to the tenets of Judaism but are also willing to declare their admiration for Jesus. The new group's formation shocked many traditionalist Jews—and others as well— but it is an understandable albeit aberrant outgrowth of the brave new world in which we find ourselves, one in which there has been a shake-up in the stratification of Americans as Jews, Catholics, and Protestants. Denominationalism has given way to interdenominationalism, and perhaps an appropriate symbol is found is the invitation sent out by intermarried parents who had been blessed with a boy-child. The couple invited their friends to a "brissening." *Bris* (or brit) is the word for the ritual circumcision of a boy.

Perhaps the world itself is undergoing a new "brissening," the emergence of people who are determined to transcend the limitations of adherence to one branch of the Judeo-Christian family.

Motivated by love, the scene may ascend to God. Those involved in intermarriages may be the harbingers of an era in which the Biblical vision of a united humanity may be realized. Even if one of the partners does not shift to the faith of his spouse, propinquity itself will make that individual more knowledgeable of, and therefore more sympathetic and less hostile to the religious outlook of his neighbors.

Every person married to someone of another faith becomes a living bridge between the traditions of his ancestors and the traditions of his spouse. The marriage itself will therefore encounter complexities galore, but in the long run it may contribute to a reduction of internecine strife among monotheistic religions. Such a trifle as the goodies which a Jewish mother-in-law makes for her Christian son-in-law may pave the path for greater tolerance and understanding. Wasn't it Harry Golden who said that the key to the solution of antisemitism is Jewish food?

As we have indicated, there has been a recent influx of non-Jews into Judaism. These newcomers have been drawn into the Jewish orbit primarily through matrimony. A notable example is the late Mrs. Michel, the granddaughter of a Yale University president and the daughter of a Vassar president. Before her death in an air crash, Mrs. Michel became one of the leaders of the American Jewish community, occupying the post, among others, of Chairman of the Board of the American College in Jerusalem.

On the other side of the coin, the record contains many Jews who passed over into Christianity. A brief roster of families which were originally Jewish but which are no longer so includes such familiar names as the Schlesingers, the Erlichmanns, the Jaworskis, and the Goldwaters. As a matter of fact, a case can be made for the contention that had there been a rabbinic "intermarrier" in Arizona two generations ago the Goldwaters would have remained Jewish. The story goes that the Senator's father, then named Goldwasser, came to Arizona after a California period and set up shop, i.e., a department store. Barry, born Baruch, fell in love with an Episcopalian young lady from Chicago and, when they decided on marriage, both would have been hospitable to a Jewish ceremony. But there was no rabbi in the vicinity, let alone a Jewish clergyman who at that time would have joined a Jew and an unconverted non-Jew. An Episcopalian priest joined the pair, who then gravitated towards Episcopalianism. True, there are those who would deem this a gain for the Jews and not a loss, but there are others who would think otherwise. One recalls two other Harry Golden quips. One was uttered at the time of the nomination: "I knew the first Jewish president would be an Episcopalian." The other came during the campaign: "The initials of the candidates should be reversed because Goldwater is LBJ (a little bit Jewish) and Johnson is BG (a big gentile)."

The situation does indeed offer "food for thought."

The Future:
Can Intermarriages
Be Made to Work?

A wit once said that the principal cause of divorce is marriage. If there were no marriages there would be no divorces. Perhaps there should be fewer marriages, considering how vulnerable many unions are.

Who was it who first observed that instead of a marriage license costing a few dollars and a divorce costing a few thousand, it ought to be the other way around?

We do live in a permissive age and there are prophets who say that marriage is doomed. The astonishing thing therefore is how well the institution of marriage has continued to flourish. Overall, the one-to-one arrangement seems to be the best for a man and a woman. The family is here to stay, or perhaps it is here to sway, but it is doing well.

And, by and large, marital fidelity is the norm, although one of Louis Nizer's favorite stories is a commentary on that phenomenon. The famed attorney likes to tell about the woman in a divorce suit who was charged with infidelity and responded: "I have so been faithful to my husband. I was faithful hundreds of times."

What is required to make an intermarriage operable?

First, what is required is what makes *any* marriage work. If you want to make your marriage work, you have to work. You have to work at it.

Not so many years ago divorce was something scandalous which most respectable people shunned. Couples would go out of their way to conceal any tension between them. Even though the Anglican Church was built on the basis of man's right to be liberated from his wife, the head of the Anglican church, King Edward, had to give up his throne when he fell in love with a woman who had been divorced. The current Queen of England's sister was said to have married not her first choice, but her second, because Man No. 1 in her life had been divorced. It has been said that Adlai Stevenson's chances of becoming president of the U.S. were hurt by the fact that he was a divorced man. And others say Nelson Rockefeller would have been in the White House were it not for his divorce.

Now the pendulum has swung the other way; the unthinkable has become commonplace. Whether the mode was started or highlighted by Nelson Rockefeller or not, in the last decade the divorce rate has soared. As a consequence, many couples will "split" at the drop of a hat or whenever the temperature of their passion undergoes a slight drop.

The surge towards divorce may have been accelerated by the advent of the Fords into the White House. Gerald

Ford (ne King) has divorced parents. His wife, Betty, was once divorced, and her spectacular comment on a television show that divorces might be reduced if young people (such as her then 18-year-old daughter) were to indulge in illicit liaisons probably advanced permissiveness several degrees.

Since divorces are so numerous, it is inevitable that many couples enter matrimony not with the feeling that they are assuming permanent obligations but with a casualness which makes them susceptible to thoughts of severance at the first quarrel.

So, independent of the nature of the marriage, whether it be of those who are "like" or those who are "unlike," the union is only as strong as the desire of the pair to keep it strong.

As a rule of thumb, the proposition that one family is just large enough for one faith is valid and most helpful. So, if it is an interfaith marriage, the chances of its success will be greater, as we have said, if the partner with less piety crosses over to the other's religion.

If the devoutness of each of the pair is low, the scene is set for an interesting adventure: let them "shop" religions. Each week, let them visit the worship gatherings of various groups and see whether they are attracted to any of them. If one religion seems especially appealing, the couple might do well to become affiliated with that particular denomination.

The exploration could include chats with various religious leaders. All clergymen are anxious to dispense infor-

mation about their outlook; they would welcome an in-
quiring couple who came to challenge them as to why
"we should join up with you."

Naturally, the inquiry could include not only visits to
various sanctuaries and talks with ministers, but also some
reading. Anything the couple does in tandem strengthens
companionability and makes for a stronger bond that is
able to resist possible future erosion.

If the couple decides that each should retain their own
religion it should be clear in advance that the process is
quite like walking a tightrope. It can be done, of course,
but it requires much sensitivity and never-ceasing vigi-
lance.

Such marriages have prospered, and anyone reading this
could cite examples. One that comes to my mind is that
of a couple I know in Florida. She is a pillar of the Episcopalian Church; he is a trustee of a synagogue. In this case
they have no children, so that complication is absent. This
couple intervisit religiously; she often goes to synagogue
and he accompanies her frequently to her worship services.
The rector and the rabbi are among their best friends and
they entertain them often, frequently at the same time.

Another piquant case is that of a mixed couple who
have four children. Two of them were sent to the Catholic
church; the other two were enrolled in the temple school.
It worked somehow, and the home was a busy place where
comparative religion was the order of the day. However,
this requires an agility that most of us cannot muster.

The seemingly ideal and ostensibly idyllic way of
handling the matter of raising children if you are part of

a mixed marirage is to expose them to the religious teachings of the spectrum of churches and synagogues and then let them "decide for themselves" in which direction to go. I have never heard of this working successfully. Children are more comfortable if they grow up naturally in one religious environment and, as I have said before, are no more capable of deciding on how to say their prayers than they are on what to eat or what to wear in their early years. The parents should decide for themselves where they want to go religiously, if anywhere, and then mold the youngsters in accordance with that mutually-arrived-at choice.

In the case of an intermarriage, the temptation is great to drift religiously. When children come, they too are permitted to drift. This may prove workable but it is not pleasant in neighborhoods where, as indicated previously, children are expected to be able to answer the question, "What are you?" In such an environment, the youngster whose answer must be "Nothing," is liable to be traumatized. The extent of religious zeal is not as important, in such cases, as the ability on the part of the child to come up with an easy response, and thus avoid being put down as "odd."

Since the onrush of intermarriage does not seem to be dwindling, a *modus operandi* for those couples who are involved must be eventually arrived at, or perhaps *modus vivendi* would be a better term.

It may be that those who have broken the marriage barrier, defied the past, and permitted their romantic inclinations to transcend their attachment to church and synagogue may be the trailblazers of some new forms of religious arrangements.

Historians like to point out that divergent groups have intersected in the past and have fashioned a kind of synthesis, or syncretism. Whatever the term, it will be fascinating to note the newer developments in the endeavors to make intermarriage work. Idealists of all faiths have envisioned a time when all cultural groups will merge. The prophets of old anticipated an era when all men would recognize the value and validity of acknowledging the Deity and together they would "go up to the mountain of the Lord." Many progressive Christians are calling for the "rejudaization" of Christianity, that is, a kind of re-amalgamation between the mother and daughter religions. In the Protestant churches, denominationalism is breaking down and, despite drawbacks, something called COCU (Council of Church Unity) is now regarded as less "cuckoo."

Perhaps the intermarrying couples, motivated initially by romance, will become the harbingers of a new kind of world unity, in which not only couples but ideologies and theologies will "live happily ever after."

We shall see.

Reflections of a Rabbi
Involved in Intermarriages

The novel experience of providing a Jewish ceremony for mixed couples has brought me into contact with groups and individuals who were previously not well known to me.

Since I am one of those "heretical" rabbis who performs weddings in tandem with Christian clergymen, I have frequently witnessed the rituals of my colleagues.

If they will forgive my presumptuousness, I will offer the opinion that the Christian wedding ceremonies are much too impersonal.

In Judaism we address ourselves to the people involved in all life cycles. If we do a baby-blessing, we make comments appropriate to the family situation. If we give a youngster a charge at a Bar Mitzvah or a Bat Mitzvah, we make references to the distinctive circumstances of the family. When we confirm or consecrate young people, our exercises include a statement directed to the people involved. At a funeral our eulogy alludes to the character and career of the deceased. Sometimes perhaps we are a bit fulsome, as in the fictional case of a rabbi who lauded the deceased to the skies and then looked into the coffin and exclaimed, "My God, I *know* that man!"

At a Jewish wedding it is customary for the rabbi to make comments specifically touching upon the aspirations of the parents and grandparents of the bride and groom and to exhibit an understanding of the special nature of the couple.

Christian ceremonies are often impersonal. One wedding I attended not long ago in a church (I was there as a spectator) was exceedingly elaborate. The bells rang. The ushers were elegantly attired and each guest was escorted to his seat by the ushers in formal fashion. Hundreds of dollars worth of flowers were banked on the altar of the church. The music was elaborate. The many attendants marched down the aisles in a precise, well-rehearsed manner. The attendants had been on hand the night before for a dinner and detailed "dry-run." The ceremony was executed with superb precision.

When the couple finally reached the climactic point, the ministers (there were two of them) kept their eyes on their manuals and mechanically went through the prescribed order of service without once looking up at the couple or making a single comment about the families involved. When the ceremony (which could have been on tape) was completed, the recessional exercises went off in martial style.

The sole personal element in such a ceremony (and it is the norm) is the utterance of the names of the bride and groom: "Do you, Marcia, takes Charles to be your husband," etc.

The Roman Catholic officiant sometimes offers what is called a "homily." The little talk avoids the personal. It is usually a platitudinous salute to "love," without much relevance to the families who are standing there. Nowadays, Roman Catholic priests will unbend a bit, and one of them, in my presence, said, "Actually, I should be the last person to pontificate about married life."

However, the priest could very well warm up the homily with some mention of what he knows about the couple.

Illustrative of the personal touch is what I told the eldest of my five sons when I presided at his marriage. I told him that prior to that glittering day his mother had scanned all the books of etiquette to make sure that the big event would go off in proper manner. I looked into one of those books and I read that it is the bridegroom that is obligated to give a check to the clergyman. I then said, "And since I'm the clergyman and you're the bridegroom, Lee, I expect a check from you. Oh, I'm not referring to money. What I want is a check from you on any impulse or tendency that would threaten the sweet harmony that I pray will always prevail between you and your bride." I then went on to make some brief allusions to the qualities of the couple which had endeared them to their own families and subsequently to others.

Both the Protestant and Catholic rites make use of "Biblical readings." They rarely vary. The customary reading from the "Old Testament" is the part of the Creation story in Genesis in which God asks Adam to marshall all living creatures before him and determines that none of these creatures would make a suitable helpmate. So God created woman and thereafter, to use the archaic language, man would "cleave" unto her.

The quaintly zoological nature of the reading is completely out of place in a marriage ceremony where the idea of romance should prevail.

When my Christian colleagues ask me to do a reading from the Jewish "Bible," my choice is that passage in Genesis where Jacob is described as toiling for seven years for his chosen one, "and they seemed but a few days for the love he had for her" (Gen. 20:20). Now, *that* is a romantic passage and some of my Christian clerics now use it instead of the Creation selection.

The favorite New Testament passage in the marriage manual of my Roman Catholic associates is Paul's accolade to love in I Corinthians 13, which begins "Though I speak with the tongues of men and of angels," etc. The reading includes something to the effect, "even if I give my body to burn." This has a jarring impact at a wedding and neutralizes the value of the finale: "And now abideth, faith, hope, and charity, and the greatest of these is charity," even when the minister mistranslates charity as "love."

Then there are the poetic readings which some couples like to have included in the marriage ceremonies. The most popular choice is the poet Gibran. Somewhere he has a lyrical admonition to the effect that those in love should not stand too close together, or drink from the same cup. That might be good hygiene, but is out of place at a wedding rite, especially since in the Jewish ceremony the couple does indeed drink wine from one cup. Examined closely Gibran is gibberish.

These days the couple often wants to write their own "vows" or read some poetry or have their attendants read some. All of this sounds delightful but in practice it's usually comical or disastrous.

The couple is in no condition to do any of the reading. Few are capable of the kind of vocal projection needed to make oneself audible before a large group, and, besides, they are so nervous that they read poorly or, if they have decided to commit their material to memory, will fluff their lines.

Rarely has a reading by the couple or by their attendants been audible at the many ceremonies I have attended. Either they break out into nervous giggles or people in the audience do—precisely when there should be a touch of solemnity in the air. I caution against this.

The motivation for participatory ceremonies is understandable. The Christians know that there is little that is personal in the clerical ritual; they want to "juice it up" a bit. If my Christian friends will add another Jewish ingredient to their ecclesiastical baggage (which already contains numerous loans from the Jewish faith), they will alter their ways and introduce a personal touch into the proceedings. In my case, I don't even have a book in front of me. The set parts of the ceremony I have memorized; the other parts of the ceremony I do eyeball-to-eyeball, carefully preparing my remarks.

Occasionally, I have a contretemps with Christian clergymen. For example, I think it unfair to have a mixed couple kneel. I think it deferential for the Christian minister to delete trinitarian terminology from his rite.

And, again I hope I'll be forgiven, I think it's time to eliminate the wholly artificial portion of the ceremony where the question is asked, "Who gives this bride away?" After a while, the query begins to sound puerile. It is also condescending and what is now labeled as "sexist."

Interestingly enough, this ecumenical epoch has led to the adoption by churches of some of the ingredients of the traditional Jewish ceremony. For example, in the Orthodox rite (which we Reformers often emulate) the bride does not march up to the altar only on the arm of her father, but escorted by both her parents. This is being done now frequently by Christians and is even suggested by priests and Protestant pastors, who sometimes put the question thus: "Do you want to march up the aisle Jewish style?"

The breaking of the glass at the conclusion of the ceremony has also been borrowed by Christians. The significance of that custom transcends Judaism; it is a reminder to the couple that the kind of impulsiveness suggested by stamping on the glass should be avoided, and it also somehow represents the fact that the couple must start out on a life of its own. The glass-stamping also punctuates the event and brings about a welcome transition from the solemnity of the ritual into the conviviality of the reception.

A whole cluster of occupations thrive on the sidelines of marriage. There are the florist and the caterer, the photographer and the printer and a growing new profession: the wedding specialist, an individual who will take over all of the planning for the event. The marriage specialist handles everything for a price: the invitations, the choice of a place, the arrangements for flowers and entertainment and photos and the "choreography." This is a relatively new profession, and one which is flourishing these days.

If my views are of any value, I would suggest that many weddings are "over-flowered." The banks and banks of floral decorations on the altar and on the tables often constitute an extravagant display enjoyed for but a few moments.

As for the photographers, they like me because I am one of those clergymen who doesn't mind in the least if pictures are being snapped throughout the ceremony since to me the retention of the pictures is of greater significance than the avoidance of a bit of distraction. With advanced photographic techniques, the pictures can be taken most unobtrusively. I suggest to the picture-takers that they stand in front of the couple (behind me) and thus get "shots" of their faces instead of just their backs.

Caterers are a fascinating breed. I like them for the most part. They are infinitely patient, usually most cordial, and extremely helpful. In the absence of a professional wedding arranger, the maitre d' at many places will show the families how to line up for their march and will actually play major domo, guiding the couple and the attendants and the parents and the clergyman with great efficiency and courtesy. One of my favorite quips is, "I did a wedding last week and I've never seen two happier people than the caterer and his wife."

Music enhances any ceremony, and the entertainers are uniformly gracious. I will confess that I don't care for songs during the ceremony, for we in the bridal party are standing up and it gets rather tedious just to stand there while the vocalist is singing. A song before the ceremony or one as the recessional begins is fine. Cantorial music during the rite is fine. And, of course, music at the reception is welcome, if not too raucous. What I cannot stand is music played "under" me while I am addressing the couple.

Music is best when it's "live." If it's "canned," it should be expertly managed. I must confess I have ideological qualms when the conventional wedding music by Wagner is played, since Wagner was a hater, but I try not to think about it, considering the fact that his works have become standard at so many weddings. Nor can I sympathize with the sophisticated brides who don't want to hear "Here Comes the Bride." It may not be the greatest piece of music in the world, but for me it really isn't a wedding if that selection is omitted. The most pleasant kind of wedding music is that which is played on an organ, although nowadays the flute, the cello, the guitar, and other instruments are often heard.

The details of a wedding can often lead to disputes. Sometimes the bride and her mother are at odds over some phase of the arrangements. Sometimes the two sets of parents engage in arguments over other parts of the proceedings, such as who is to be invited and where are people to be seated.

With respect to differences between the couple and their parents, I invariably plead with the couple to yield to their elders. "After all," I remonstrate, "you have each other. It's your marriage, so let your parents enjoy the wedding." Weddings are really for the families, not the couple. Hence the couple should give in when there are some variations between themselves and their parents or, in some cases, their grandparents. The magnification of trivia in wedding plans is so commonplace that one minister said, "I don't officiate at weddings. I referee."

I have one more final, perhaps revolutionary suggestion. It is the convention, as anyone knows who is properly Emily-Posted, for the bride's side to pay for the wedding. I think it is time to put an end to this one-sided arrangement. I think the time has come for both sides to share in the financing of a wedding. After all, both families are equally involved; they should be equal in underwriting the grand event. What do you think?

Index

Rumania, antisemitism in, 24
Russia, Jewish persecution in, 23

Shakespeare, 21
Sheen, Bishop Fulton, 51
Social consequences of intermarriage, 37–38

Tabernacles, 82
Talmud, 56
Taylor, Elizabeth, 33, 52

Union of American Hebrew Congregations, 84
United States, 24–25

Vatican Council, 48

War brides, 8, 15, 31
World Council of Churches in Christ, 48
World War II, religious interaction during, 47–48

Yom Kippur, 60, 61–62, 83